THE LAND QUESTION.

THE

LAND QUESTION:

AN ENQUIRY INTO THE OWNERSHIP AND TRANSFER OF LAND

AND

REFORM PROPOSALS APPLICABLE TO SCOTLAND.

BY

JOHN ERSKINE.

GLASGOW:
WILLIAM HODGE & CO., 26 BOTHWELL STREET.
1895.

PREFACE.

THE matter contained in the following pages was at first intended for a short series of articles to be published in the *Scottish Law Review*. Though it soon appeared that the subject could not be overtaken in the three or four articles beyond which the series could not be conveniently extended, the writing was continued in accordance with the original idea. The arrangement of the matter might have been different had the full scope of the enquiry been realised from the first.

I have abstained from citing the opinions of writers on the Land Question, partly because the reader may know them already, but chiefly because the views I have put forward should be taken on their own merits, and should neither be accepted because supported, nor rejected because opposed, by so-called "authorities." An authority is scarcely worthy of the name if it cannot in some way, or to some extent, enforce its views; and, so far as I know, there are, amongst writers on this subject, no such authorities. Many writers have given forth many opinions, but, for practical result, we look around in vain. For what I have written I claim no authority. I think, however, it should help others to think for themselves. And that is a great point.

JOHN ERSKINE.

151 St. Vincent Street,
    Glasgow, 1st June, 1895.

CONTENTS.

CHAPTER	PAGE
I.—Introductory,	1
II.—Consideration of Land-Reform "Principles,"	6
III.—Natural Way of Dealing with Land,	13
IV.—How Far Ancestral Arrangements Obligatory,	18
V.—Unearned Increment,	22
VI.—The Cause of the Increment and Its Ownership,	25
VII.—The Prairie-Value Principle,	31
VIII.—The Increment Further Considered,	35
IX.—Property and its Limitations,	39
X.—A Land Court and Its Functions,	45
XI.—Need of Land Court Illustrated,	52
XII.—The Tribunal,	54
XIII.—Title-Deeds and Certificates of Title,	58
XIV.—The Reformer and his Obstacles,	62

CONTENTS.

CHAPTER	PAGE
XV.—Other Obstacles to Reform,	67
XVI.—The Certificate of Title,	70
XVII.—Minor Points of Reform,	79
XVIII.—General Considerations,	84
XIX.—Taxation of Land,	88
XX.—Minerals,	94
XXI.—The Land and Population,	101
XXII.—The Land and the Game,	106
XXIII.—Primogeniture and Entail,	109
XXIV.—Casualties of Superiority,	115
XXV.—Prescription, Searches, and Records,	121
XXVI.—Some Effects of Proposed Reforms,	124
XXVII.—Conclusion,	128

THE LAND QUESTION.

Chapter I.

INTRODUCTORY.

From history, both sacred and profane, we learn that there have always been the rich and the poor, and, so far as we can gather, the inequality was for long ages regarded as incidental to mankind. Indeed it had come to be accepted as an ordinance of the Supreme Being, and that, though it might be lawful for each individual for himself to pass from poverty to wealth, it was not either lawful or hopeful to make the attempt by any sort of class combination. "The poor ye have always with you" was misread as the declaration of a necessity rather than the declaration of a fact, and, even yet, pious people (who are well off) regard the poverty of others as due to the decree of Providence. But the poor are now being told that their poverty is the result purely of misgovernment, and thus we have fallen on very different times. Now, the popular way to rise is not so much by individual effort under existing conditions as by finding out and by the removal of the obstacles to advancement due to existing conditions. Rising in the world by one's own effort is a slow process, and men are so impatient! Hence, if it can be shown that some change in the arrangements of society will benefit those who are down, it is deemed impious for those who are not down to object to the change. Even if their objection is the outcome of better knowledge and greater intelligence, it is at once branded as selfishness, and unworthy even of consideration. The discoverer of obstacles in the way of the poor man is usually not slow to publish his discovery, and, as a drowning man clutches at every straw, it is not wonderful that the discoverer has soon a great multitude of believers and followers. In a country like ours, with a democratic franchise, this is a serious matter, and, with a free press and an open platform, it is impossible to measure the influence of the "discoverer," whether he be right or wrong. Free trade was to do everything for the people; but it didn't, though it did much. Eight hours a day would, in the opinion of many, put an end to poverty; while it is a certainty with others that local option would herald the millennium. There is another and a very active and intelligent set of reformers who tell us that poverty would disappear as if by magic if the private ownership of land on present conditions were abolished, and if the "unearned increment" were appropriated to the community. Every rectification of error or abuse is beneficial and helps on the chariot of civilisation, but most advocates of rectification expect and confidently predict greater and better results than could possibly arise from the several reforms which they advocate. Unfortunately, every reform proposal is taken up without knowledge by masses who follow the leader only because he holds out prospects which, if realised, would bring advantage to those whom he leads. Unhappily also every reform interferes with vested interests, and is opposed by those who have, or fancy they have, something to lose by the proposed change. But a serious proposal made from an honest belief that it would benefit society is entitled to earnest and honest consideration, and, as we are not aware of any such treatment of the proposals of the land-reformers, we propose to devote some pages to the subject.

The defenders of the *status quo* may be reminded that it is quite conceivable that, as the child cannot manage, and the youth generally mismanages, his own affairs, so society in its childhood and youth may have made faulty arrangements in regard to the land. In early times, when land was plentiful everywhere (as it still is many a where), our ancestors were under no necessity to distinguish between land as a valuable possession, or property, and other things which were valuable possessions, or property. The land which grew the corn, equally with the corn itself, was felt to be a means of sustaining life, therefore a necessity, therefore a thing to be possessed, therefore a thing to be handed down to children, or, failing children, to those whom it was desired to benefit. The inducements to treat land like other property were thus so great as to be irresistible, and for following this natural and irresistible course the latter-day land-reformer calls his ancestors in question. He does more. He calls in question the very rights of those who to-day hold the land, and that equally whether the possession is based on inheritance or purchase. He goes back to first principles, to the best of his ability, and he finds (at least he lays it down) that land is so different in its nature from other things that it is not a fit subject of private property, that all that a man can own in the land is what he puts on it or into it by his own labour, and that he must give up to the community that adventitious increase in the value which has been christened the "unearned increment." These first principles, as he proudly calls them, have a certain charm of simplicity, they look incontrovertible, and, what is perhaps more to the purpose, they look promising. Armed with a principle, especially a first principle, the reformer is certain of victory, and does not hesitate to trample upon anything that opposes his triumphal progress.

Let us pause to ask, What is a principle? It is an abstract proposition which is quite harmless and quite useless till applied to some human affairs. You might carry on an academic discussion about it till Doomsday without finding out the soundness or unsoundness of the principle in any way that would be authoritative. But stop the discussion and apply the principle to the matter which it is supposed to regulate and you will soon know whether it is sound or unsound, sense or nonsense. From a harmless abstract proposition it will rise, for some, to the rank of a sublime truth, and fall, for others, to the level of a damnable heresy. It is like Carlyle's definition of orthodoxy and heterodoxy—"my doxy and thy doxy." Perhaps principles, especially reformers' principles, should be more carefully examined than they usually are, and subjected to the same test as trees and men: "by their fruits ye shall know them." A principle manufactured for the occasion is like a definition; it may contain all, but it cannot contain more than you know of the subject, and that may be the whole or it may be only a part. The man who manufactures a principle always confounds it with an axiom, and those who accept the principle generally make the same mistake. When the principle happens to be nonsense (as so many so-called principles are) there is very little chance that those who adopt it will escape unsound conclusions. As the land-reformer abounds in principles, and asks nothing which his principles do not warrant, perhaps we should begin our enquiry by an examination of some of his principles.

Chapter II.

CONSIDERATION OF LAND-REFORM "PRINCIPLES."

"Land is not a fit subject of private property." This is the land-reformer's leading principle, and it looks like an axiom when propounded in the heart of Glasgow, where ground is sold by the yard like silk or velvet. Carry the principle to the moors of Argyleshire, the inhospitable islands of the Hebrides, or the prairies of America, and somehow it loses its force and also its importance. An axiom does not vary in that way. The principle under consideration is not old, and it is town-bred. It could scarcely have had its birth in the country, but if born there it must have had a city man for its father. To drop metaphor and deal in fact, this principle is the outcome of high prices of city lots and of the large incomes of great landowners. It has therefore a suspicious resemblance to the protest of a man who wants land and can't get it on as easy terms as he would like. But many land-reformers have no personal purpose to serve, unless it be to gratify their feelings of sympathy with others who want land and cannot obtain it. The principle is therefore not to be discredited except on its own merits.

So far as we know, the colonisation of the world

(which has now made some way in certain parts, but none at all in other parts) was very slow and gradual, and always radiated from a centre outwards. When the adoption of a new centre occurred soon enough, and when the radiation therefrom went on quickly enough, there was no land question we may be sure. But such adoption and radiation involved a good deal of sacrifice, or at all events of uncertainty. Men did not like to leave the cultivated field for the prairie, not even if the new land was a land of promise. "We rather bear those ills we have than fly to others that we know not of." Sentiment aggravated the difficulty. "There is no place like home." The father of the family, when he had to leave the family home at the call of death, naturally left it to the eldest of his sons, from whom he had longest received help to cultivate his fields and reap his harvests. The law of primogeniture may be ever so bad and deserving of abolition, but it was the natural way. We can fancy younger brothers, especially if unmarried, preferring service with, and some measure of subordination to, the elder brother rather than extrusion from the family home, and that more especially if the portion of the younger sons was small and their ambition was not great. But these arrangements, after being made and working smoothly for a time, would by and by be found to be unsuitable and deficient in expansiveness in the case of increasing population. Even if the elder brother consented to sub-division of the inherited land, the expedient would be only a temporary relief, and with a further increase of the population, the congestion, as we call it, would recur worse than ever. Jacob must have seemed to Esau a sort of land-grabber, and that was perhaps why he stood in need of police protection for a time. We imagine Esau grudged his brother not so much the paternal blessing as the paternal acres. If this is so, the land question is not new. Perhaps the way out of the difficulty is the old way of radiation and new centres. Perhaps the evil of which the land-reformer complains is due to the obstinacy with which mankind refuses to obey the old command or accept the standing invitation to go in and possess the land. Men want to possess the bits that are already possessed. They naturally prefer, when hungry, a bushel of corn to the land that produces it, just as one would prefer a sovereign to the ore in the mine which contains an equal weight of the metal.

As the land-reformer goes back to first principles, so must we. But, as hinted above, principles are to be tried by their fitness for circumstances. The principle which does not fit circumstances is not a principle but an arbitrary dictum drawn from incomplete data, or, in other words, is the pronouncement of ignorance mistaking itself for superior knowledge. Now, on what principle should a pioneer of civilization (or cultivation, which is sometimes the same thing) deal with the land he has reclaimed from prairie when he is unable any longer to use it? Provided he did not dispossess a former occupant by force or fraud, it scarcely matters how he got the land—whether by simple appropriation or by concession from the governing authority. If he found no one else wanting the land, or took no unfair advantage of competitors for it, then, when he is done with it, living or dying, he will have the inclination to hand it over to his family, or to a purchaser, to the exclusion of all others whether regarded as individuals or as society. Is there any sound reason why this pioneer should not follow his inclination? In the case we are dealing with there does not appear to be any one, or any body of persons, with the right to interfere. Nobody but the pioneer did anything for the land, or, during his occupancy, could lawfully, *i.e.*, reasonably, have interfered with his possession, provided that, if he held the land by concession, he fulfilled the conditions of the grant. He had gone in and possessed the land in question and left others free to go in and possess other land. In a very thinly populated country this pioneer might have no other way of disposing of his land than to leave it to his family. A purchaser might be an impossibility, either because people were too scarce or land was too plentiful. But if his family circumstances did not secure transmission by inheritance, the alternative of transmission by sale was lawful and reasonable, and, assuming a buyer to have been found, the title by purchase would be good. If the title of this first purchaser was good, what can be said against the title of subsequent purchasers acquiring in accordance with the law of the country? For the present purpose we do not need to distinguish among different forms of government in order to ascertain the measure of respect due to the law, nor, if only a democratic government is thought worthy of respect, need we enquire in the case of a democracy when it emerged out of some earlier or less popular form of government. If it is unjust or contrary to sound policy to-day for a great landowner to draw enormous revenues from ground in the heart of a city, when did it become unjust or contrary to sound policy to allow the land-owner to reap the profits obtainable from his land? If the city had grown eastwards and not westwards and had left this land-owner's land at its old agricultural value, his revenues would not have attracted attention. But the growth of the city was in his direction, and we have to find the point at which his profits from that growth should have stopped. The ground he holds to-day is the ground his predecessor in the title bought from the pioneer, or the pioneer's son or successor.

If, as the land-reformer alleges, land is not a fit subject of private property, the pioneer's possession of the land which he cleared must have been wrong, or when he was done with it the transmission of it to his heir or to the purchaser must have been wrong. Was either of these wrong? The land-reformer has not directed his objection to this case, but perhaps he should. If he goes on first principles, he might do well to go also on primary conditions of human affairs, out of which his client, known by the name of "society," has been evolved. Deny the pioneer right to bequeath or sell his "clearance," his property in land as he would call it, and you take away the motive to convert the prairie into cultivated fields. Like the patriarchs of the Old Testament, his wealth consists in lands and flocks and herds, and if he cannot dispose of these as he pleases he is reduced to the level of what we know as a crofter, drawing a bare subsistence from the land he tills, and tilling (or allowed to till) only enough to keep soul and body together. The crofter is not the highest type of man, and it is not surely the policy of any set of reformers to multiply the crofter class as we know them. But it is idle to discuss whether the pioneer should be allowed to transmit his land to his heir or to a purchaser, for, in his circumstances, he would have little or no choice. We are not restricted to ancient or patriarchal days for illustrations of the position and circumstances of the pioneer. In our own day in America, and in some of our own colonies, the pioneer is to be found under the very conditions we have been dealing with. Is the title of these men good to-day, and is it to become bad in their own hands, or in the hands of their successors (in the title) to-morrow, or next day, or next year, or next century? If it is not a good title that will remain a good title for better for worse, that is for rise or for fall in value, the sooner the fact is announced the better for all parties—the pioneer, the heir, the purchaser, and society. The case we have taken by which to test the fitness of land to be treated as private property does appear to show that the land is not to be distinguished from the flocks and herds, or the implements of husbandry, or the house on the land, or the furniture in the house, when any question of property is raised, and that equally whether for possession or transmission by inheritance or purchase.

Chapter III.

NATURAL WAY OF DEALING WITH LAND.

IF, like the Sabbath, the earth was made for man, it is natural and reasonable that he should desire to have and to hold it in accordance with his necessities and his habits. The primary necessities are food and shelter, and, nomads notwithstanding, the leading habit is to attach himself to a particular place and call it "home." A primary necessity of the race, though only an instinct of the individual, is to propagate the species—to multiply and replenish the earth. These necessities and habits cannot be left out of view when the land question is under consideration. There is on this question, as well as on many others, a tendency on the part of some to reason and to legislate for men, as if mankind were different from what they are and have always been and, so far as we can see, will for ever remain. Mankind has two very different sets of desires—those that are natural and proper, and those that are natural (though sometimes called unnatural) and improper. The first are to be recognised and provided for, while the second are to be recognised and denied. One common, if not universal, desire of civilized man is to have a spot of earth which he can call home, and his own. That is a desire which is both natural and proper, and the gratification of which, as our pioneer illustration showed, is not contrary to first principles. Indeed, human nature being what it is, first principles seem to require that a man shall be allowed to keep the land which he has brought under cultivation. His possessory right must imply the right to alienate for love, favour, and affection, or for a price or other valuable consideration. Deny him this right and you take away the motive to do more than coax the land, in return for the least possible cultivation, to yield a bare subsistence to the incumbent for the time being. On this condition the material progress of the world would be slow and small, and the consequences of this condition would be far-reaching and tremendous. One would scarcely care to live with the sort of men whom this state of matters would produce. There might be none in absolute want, but there would be none, or at least few, above the rank of the labourer as we know him. It would be a humdrum sort of world, saved perhaps from the reproach of a workhouse, but wanting in all the products of art, literature, and science, and without a trace of those things which only wealth and leisure can produce. It may be proof of a serious flaw and defect in human nature, but it is pretty certain that, constituted as we are, nothing but the hope of future ease and luxury in some one of its many forms would tempt men to exert themselves beyond the point of securing the bare necessaries of life. Perhaps our ancestors have not blundered after all in their land-law arrangements. The pioneer illustration does not exhaust the case. Let us repeat in passing, for what it is worth, that in our own day absolute proprietorship in the land is being conferred upon the pioneer class, not in one country only but in many. The land-law reformer will tell you that the repetition of a wrong does not make it right: and neither it does. But the persistence in a course suggests that there are reasons for it which, if not satisfactory to the individual, seem to be sufficient to the race. The individual, though, is sometimes right where the race is wrong. It therefore will not do to take anything for granted.

We have admitted that the pioneer illustration does not exhaust the case. Land has been made the property of the individual under very different circumstances from those of the pioneer. The king has, in days gone by, bestowed large, sometimes enormous, tracts of land on Court favourites. The bestowal was open to two observations: first, The land did not belong to the king; second, The favourites were perhaps the least deserving people who could have been found for the favour. There is not much in the second observation, though it is usually more emphasised than the first. If the community is wronged by the gift, the evil lies not in the selection of the donee but in the deprivation of those whom the donee keeps out of their rights. But so far as history informs us, the donee did not deprive the community or cultivators of their rights as they understood them, but rather became the guardian of those rights and the champion of their holders. For illustration, take a great Scottish noble and landowner whose grant of land was under the condition that, in the King's cause, he would bring a certain number of armed men into the field when required. In the circumstances of the times the return which the noble had to make for his grant of land was a *reddendo* quite equivalent to the benefit conferred upon him. He had so to arrange the affairs of his vassals that they would be able to take the field when he sent round the fiery cross, and for this purpose he had to take care that they were neither without food nor without the implements of war, which, in a certain sense, may be called articles of luxury. Moreover, he had to place his own life at the mercy of war chances, in wars about which he was perhaps not consulted. The King was as much a creature of circumstances as the noble and his vassals. In this way only was it open to the King to keep his throne or to defend his kingdom against the foe who would not only have wrested from him the crown, but also from his people the land from which they drew their living. Situated as they were, the King, nobles, and people had, or knew, no other way of combining for the preservation of their position, and rights, and very life, individual and national. The land was thus dealt with in accordance with the circumstances of the times, suitably to the ideas of the men of the time. From these men and these times we inherit much. For the most part we have reason to be grateful to our ancestors. At all events we boast plenty of the " good old times," and of the glorious things done by those who have gone before. Shall we inherit the good and not also the evil ? If they made mistakes, shall we claim the rectification of these mistakes, and a return to first principles, if only we can show that, however a minority would be injured, the majority would gain ?

Chapter IV.

HOW FAR ANCESTRAL ARRANGEMENTS OBLIGATORY.

Once we let in this idea, this plan of (what some would call) correcting errors in the social arrangements of our forefathers, where would it end? None but a prophet, an Isaiah, or more probably a Jeremiah, could tell us. The land is not by any means the only thing that would require rearrangement. Everything that has led to the advantage of a few at the cost of the many might, on the same ground, be upset on pretence of being readjusted. Everything that has made the fortune of one man would be challenged on the ground that, if he had not obtained the special opportunity of which he availed himself, some other two or more might have divided amongst them what went into his private pocket. "The greatest good of the greatest number" principle might easily be strained to take from one and give to more than one, and if that principle was not found sufficient for the occasion some other principle would be found, and if none could be found one could be easily invented to serve the purpose. As an *ultima ratio*, if none better could be found, the reformer could fall back on the principle that no man shall be allowed to gain at the cost of others. The "others" would be unanimous in supporting this doctrine, and having such an overwhelming majority in its favour it would be established by that general consensus of opinion against which nothing can hold up its head in these days. It is never difficult to obtain a consensus of opinion in favour of any view that seems to favour the interests of the majority, though, on a closer view, and in the long run, it would be found that it only *seemed* to do so. Perhaps the day may come when the eldest child of the man who leaves £10,000 amongst his five children will think he has a grievance against the four younger children for robbing him of the £8000 which they take amongst them. The eldest child is distinctly damnified by the birth and survivance of the other four, and if he claim justice, *i.e.*, the whole £10,000, he will find plenty of well-principled people, perhaps suffering similarly, to support his claim.

Perhaps as we owe our existence to our ancestors and, in great measure, our physical constitution to our parents, we must be content to inherit the social and legal conditions which they bequeathed to us. They have left us scope enough, in ways innumerable, even if we accept the rights of property as sent down to us. Up till now there has not been any suggestion that we should take the movable property of our predecessors and reject the conditions under which it descends to us. But the reformer has been eloquent and profound in drawing the distinction between land and chattels. The distinction is as great and as obvious as the difference between a horse and a cart, but no greater, on a question of property. On the ground of the difference the land-law reformer asks us to go great lengths. In particular, he asks us to say that one generation has no right whatever to decide how the next generation shall deal with the land, though the owner of the horse and cart may, *mortis causa,* dispose of both just as he pleases. By fixing attention on the differences between land on the one hand, and the horse and cart on the other hand, it is easy to lay down, as the land-reformer does, one law for the land and another for the chattels. But if he would only take the trouble to regard the points of resemblance, nay, the points of identity, he would find that land and chattels have value only as they minister to the wants of man, and from this point of view the chattels in question would have no value if the land on which the horse walks and the cart stands did not go with them. A favourite argument is that man did not create the land. Is it not a fair answer that neither did he create the horse? No doubt he made the cart, but not the wood and iron of which it consists. Even reformers are apt to regard what tends to support their argument, and to pass over what makes for the opposite view. Perhaps the real question at issue is this: Is land in its very nature so different from the other things that minister to man's support that, unlike other possessions or property, it must in justice revert to the race when given up by the individual? If it does, or should, revert, then it is different from all other things called property which descend to the heirs of the individual holder. And if land cannot justly descend to the heirs of the holder, neither can that holder be allowed to defraud the race by selecting the individual who shall next enjoy it, not even if that individual bribe him with what we call a price. Either land is property or it is not property. If it is property, then the owner has a perfect right to sell or bequeath it as he pleases. If it is not property, then the community is defrauded every hour the occupier draws benefits from it and retains them for his own behoof. We have tried above to show that land is a fit subject of private property, and, in order to make progress with our argument, we must be allowed to assume that the point is proved, or conceded, if only for the sake of argument.

CHAPTER V.

UNEARNED INCREMENT.

BUT it is quite conceivable, though land may conveniently be treated as private property in primitive times, and for a limited time, that yet it is essentially the inheritance of the human race and must belong to, and be dealt with as the property of, the community, sooner or later. This view would at once open up the enquiry: At what point of the individual proprietorship must it be broken off in favour of ownership by the community? Is it something in the circumstances of the individual owner, or something in the circumstances of the community, that is to fix the *terminus ad quem* of the private owner and the *terminus a quo* of the public landlord? The land-reformer appears to fix the *terminus ad quem* only by finding out the desirable *terminus a quo*. These are not two *termini* with separate and independent existence, but only one terminus, which is both a destination and a starting point. This point is the emergence of the unearned increment. This increment is not a thing of instantaneous birth, but is rather a thing of slow growth. Like the shower, it comes from every point of the compass. Like a thief, it cometh by night. Like the pestilence, it walketh by day. Like the wind, it bloweth where it listeth, and thou hearest the sound thereof, but canst not tell whence it cometh or whither it goeth. People talk of it familiarly, but they know very little about it, and they have no control over its creation and still less over its distribution. The only thing they know about it is that it is nobody's, but everybody's. "Nobody" is easily defined, but "everybody" is more troublesome. In this sense "anybody" is not recognised as part of "everybody," yet "everybody" may be made up of anybody plus anybody. It does not matter much to whom the advantage goes if only it is taken from the man who would have kept it but for the discovery that the increment has emerged. The emergence proves to the satisfaction of the land-law reformer that it was "unearned" in every case of land; but in all other cases, such as railway shares, pictures, or "cornered" copper, it is taken for granted that the increased value is due to the sagacity of the investor, the buyer, or the cornerer, and therefore is his lawful gain. For every man who owns land there are thousands who own chattels. Is it possible that the disproportion has anything to do with the modern doctrine of the unearned increment? If it has, it is a dangerous doctrine, for the reason that it could, without much trouble, be extended to chattels, the owners of which, to any great value, are not one in a thousand to those who have no chattels of value. The unearned increment requires more careful definition and consideration than it usually receives. But we do not require to trouble ourselves with the matter unless it be either established, or conceded for the sake of argument, that land is not a fit subject of private property. We hold that it is a fit subject of private property, but to open up the argument we concede that it isn't—for the moment.

Broadly stated, the unearned increment is the increase in value so far as not caused by the act or labour of the owner. Stated affirmatively, it is the increase which arises from the action of the community in the pursuit of its own ends and without any intention of conferring advantage on the landowner.

Chapter VI.

THE CAUSE OF THE INCREMENT AND ITS OWNERSHIP.

IN some departments of human affairs, specially of human action, intention is everything and result nothing, or next to nothing. For instance, in theft the *animus furandi* is the essential element. In murder the killing is not enough without the desire, or at least the willingness, to kill. In the construction of a will intention is held to be everything and phraseology almost nothing. In those acts of the community (composed, let us remember, of individuals) done in pursuance of individual gain, there is no intention of increasing the value of the land held by their neighbours, and no idea of making up any decrease in value that may be caused by those acts. Judged by the test of intention we may conclude that the increase in value not having been meant by those who helped to create it, that increase is a thing for which they are not accountable, with which they have no concern, to which they have no right, and over which they have no control. The whole circumstances exclude the contention that, having created the increase, the community must be held to have intended to retain and are entitled to retain it for their own behoof. Each personal (as distinguished from communal) act of each individual forming the community was dictated by an exclusive regard to his own interests, and a total forgetfulness of the interests both of other individuals and the community. The individual, though held responsible by the community for his acts in some cases where others are injured by them, is allowed to retain the profit that arises from such acts if no one can show that he is wronged thereby. The damnification requires to arise from some act not within the legal right of the performer of that act. And when there is responsibility it is limited to direct results, and consequential damages are refused. The unearned increment doctrine is out of accord with all these principles, and is indeed the introduction of a principle at variance with the rules of law which regulate all other affairs. But the newness of the principle must not be allowed to procure its rejection without a fair trial in open court, if not in actual practice.

We have no pioneer land-owners in this country, nor any living donee of the Crown holding land received for nothing or a consideration less (in the sense of being worse) than nothing. The new doctrine, if applied at all, would have to be applied to land bought and paid for by the present owner, or inherited, and to that case (treating purchase and inheritance as conferring the same right) we shall apply the test by which to judge it. In the first place, a buyer of land looks carefully to its situation and surroundings. It is not to be said that a buyer sees all the things that will in the years to come tend to make his purchase more or less valuable. The seller does not see them all, and the buyer cannot be credited with foreknowledge, though it is not reasonable to suppose that he did not fix the price he would pay after due consideration of the possibilities of the land. The new doctrine would deprive him of the benefit of his sagacity in the transaction.

A land-owner, if he is a man of even common prudence, is influenced by his anticipations of future developments in the use he makes of his land, and in the expenditure of capital by which he seeks to make the most of its capabilities. He reckons not only on what he does, but also on what the community will likely do, to raise the value of his land in respect of revenue and also of capital, or selling price. But the community is not in any sense his partner in the adventure, for, if he sustain loss instead of securing gain, the community will leave him to bear it alone. And quite properly too, for the essence of partnership is the sharing of profit or loss, whichever may come, in proportions previously arranged or equally in the absence of contrary agreement. The profit on land would, under the new doctrine, go to a partner who comes forward only to take that profit, who would have kept in the background had there been no profit, who would not have subscribed a penny to make up the decrement had loss arisen, and who neither intentionally nor consciously did anything whatever to create the increment. This sleeping partner who wakens only to the sound of profit is not to be put off with a share of that profit. He is to get the whole of it because it was "unearned" by the (so-called) owner. The man who tried to earn something is held to have earned nothing, and the public which did not try to earn anything is to be held to have earned everything. In the matter of this profit the public toiled not, neither did it spin. But the man who did toil and spin is to get nothing, chiefly because he was not Robinson Crusoe, and his land was not part of an uninhabited island. The owner, had he been a pioneer, would have been welcome to his increment, not so much on account of what he had done as because there would have been nobody at hand to pretend that he had helped to bring about the improvement in value.

One of the most troublesome details in regard to the unearned increment is the point of time at which it shall be held to have come into existence. If applied to the case of the pioneer the new doctrine is manifestly absurd, though when applied to the case of land rendered very valuable by the growth of a great city it commends itself to the reformer who takes it up on the strength of a principle which appears impregnable. Nay, it is found troublesome to answer even by those who do not adopt the doctrine, for it has a kind of specious look of fairness about it. Why should Lord B make a fortune merely because the growth of the city happened to be in the direction of his land, whereas if the city had extended in the opposite direction only, or had not extended at all, he would have had little or no increase of his agricultural rents of 50 or 100 years ago? Of two who are grinding at the mill, why should one be taken and the other left? Why is A little and B tall? Why was it fine yesterday and wet to-day? Why, in short, does Providence permit so many departures in human affairs from the rule of dull unvarying uniformity? And why will those who are less fortunate always envy those who are more fortunate, and refuse to see that the fruits of the good fortune should follow the good fortune? There is in the human mind a faculty for seeing things in the light most favourable to self. The dullest intelligence is quite able to put the case for its owner with a clearness, fulness, and even acuteness that are often remarkable, and sometimes astonishing. The case of Lord B is not the best by which to judge the doctrine, though it is the one to which the "reformers" most frequently allude. The pioneer case does not suit them, yet it may be reasonable to require of them a principle or rule that will apply to every case of unearned increment. The rule, if it was properly worded, would catch the increment before it had gone too far, but without being too soon to prevent its coming into existence. It might be quite possible by, so to speak, shaking the doctrine in the face of a land-owner to deter him from doing those very things on, and with, his land which form the first and true causes of the growth of the city in his direction. For example, an owner of land may build himself a fine house on his own property, and this house may be so much admired, and its situation so much coveted, that others may feu his ground for the building of more houses, till there is quite a suburb set up. Then it may become the fashion to have a house in that suburb, and then the rate of feu-duty will go up, and the unearned increment begin to show its head. What is the true origin of this increment, and when did it have its true beginning? When the owner of the land built his own house it was not, and when the one hundredth house was put up it was. At what point between had this unearned increment its birth, and who is to find and fix that point? It must be found and fixed, otherwise by enforcing the doctrine in the case just indicated we would be open to the reproach that we had one law for the rich and another for the poor. The usual inequality would, however, be inverted, for in this case the rich would be punished while the poor would escape. The earlier and smaller increment would not be challenged, and the comparatively poor land-owner would be exempt from the operation of the confiscatory law, while Lord B and the like would be caught by it.

Chapter VII.

THE PRAIRIE-VALUE PRINCIPLE.

The land-law reformer has a principle by the remorseless application of which the point we have just discussed would be settled. The principle is that all value in excess of prairie value belongs to the community. For the proper understanding of the principle we must first enquire into this prairie value. What is it, and is it an unvarying quantity? But first of all let us notice that the principle itself negatives the very doctrine which the same reformers lay down, viz., the doctrine that land is not a fit subject of private property. If a man is able to hold on to a piece of land, and to transmit it both *inter vivos* and *mortis causa*, both gratuitously and for a valuable consideration, he is in every sense of the word the proprietor of the land no matter how you may tax him for it. It is no answer to this argument to say that the so-called owner is allowed to deal only with that value which the land had before it was reclaimed from its state of nature. The land is held in his case in perpetual lease to the exclusion of all other offerers, and a lease for even 999 years is not regarded as very different from a feu for ever. In a crowded country, and in the most crowded part of that country, who shall say what may be the value of a plot of land taxed even to the whole amount of what is thought to be the unearned increment? If there is any other one person desirous of possessing the land on the same conditions and excluded by the man in possession and his heirs and assignees, the man in possession is the owner of the land—the reformer and his reformation notwithstanding. The preference which the owner has secured over the rest of the community in regard to his bit of land must be a fraud on the community, for it contravenes the doctrine of the reformers as to the ownership of land. The doctrine is not saved by taxing the land so as to leave the owner nothing but what is called land value. Tax him as you may, the doctrine is infringed if he can sit there in spite of everybody and choose his own successor to succeed him when he is living or after he is dead. If land is not a fit subject of private property the possessor of it must relax his hold when he ceases to use the land for cultivation, for residence, or for the carrying on of business, and certainly at latest when death takes hold of him. In other words, if the land belongs to the community the community must exercise some act of ownership occasionally, and at all events as often as the fee is vacant by the death of the vassal—to borrow a phrase from the feudal law. After all, the reformer is not proposing to alter the land laws: he is only proposing to transfer taxes to land and to take them off other things.

Now, let us see what right the community has to all land values in excess of prairie value. No one can deny that but for the presence of "the community" the land held by any one man would have far less value than it acquires by the existence and growth of the community. But, unfortunately for the argument of the reformer, the same thing can be said *mutatis mutandis* of every other kind of property except, perhaps, the food by which one man proposes to sustain his own life for the next few days or weeks. The proximity of those who covet a man's possessions, or the increase in the number of the covetous, cannot lower his right to these possessions, much less extinguish his right to any part of them. Nor does it alter the case if those who claim (or covet) part of the possessions rest their claim on their alleged share in creating the value of the thing to be shared. An unintentional benefaction is not a thing for which the beneficiary requires to say "thank you," but, on the prairie-value principle, he must do far more: he must return it. In doing so, he is not to be allowed to ask the community whether it is the same community whose action produced the "increment." If it is not the same, it is the lineal successor, and, says the reformer, takes up the rights of its ancestor by way of implied special service, expede, extracted, recorded, and made effectual by virtue of the "principle" without petition, proof, or palaver of any kind. In claims of damages, we have been accustomed to the refusal of "consequential" damages on the ground that they could not have been in the view of the party whose conduct (or misconduct) produced the loss for which the consequential damages were claimed. In fixing the increment there is to be no distinction between "direct" and "consequential," intentional and unintentional, voluntary and involuntary, selfish and unselfish, foreseen and unforeseen. Every act and every omission of the community, past and present, is to be taken as having caused and produced the value in excess of prairie value, and, *quoad excessum*, off it goes to the community. Whoever has right to it, the one man called the owner has not, for, had he been the sole inhabitant of the island, the increment had never occurred. That is sufficient on which to base the judgment adverse to the owner, and, if it hardly justify the judgment in favour of the community, it scarcely matters. The successful litigant seldom finds fault with the grounds of judgment.

Chapter VIII.

THE INCREMENT FURTHER CONSIDERED.

If the unearned-increment principle is sound, it will have some expansiveness in it, and will be capable of general if not universal application. If it is otherwise, we had better beware of it. The shares of a railway company stood ten years ago at par, but, through good trade and the popularity of the line, the company has so prospered that to-day the shares stand at 50 per cent. premium, and the dividends are 6 per cent. A fire insurance company has had few losses and good business, and its dividends are 10 per cent., and its shares sell at more than double their nominal value. A typewriter costs its maker say £4 18s. 9d. to produce, but he holds a patent for its manufacture, and he easily gets £20 for it from the public. These are all cases of unearned increment arising from the existence of a community and the action of that community. If the shareholders of the railway and insurance companies and the maker of the typewriter had been the sole inhabitants of the island, the shares in the companies and the price of the typewriter would have been very different. It is dangerous to interfere with the principle that profits, like losses, must lie where they light. On the one hand, it must be admitted that the increment is "unearned" in the sense in which the land-reformer uses the expression, *i.e.*, the increment is not caused by the owner. On the other hand, it cannot be admitted that therefore the benefit arising from the increment should be taken away from the owner and given to the whole community, which includes those persons whose action and enterprise brought about the rise in value, and many more persons who had no hand in the matter beyond what is implied in living within a certain though unknown radius of the property.

The commoner type of reformer (in any department) scoffs at the vested interests which stand in the way of his proposals, though he may have little or nothing to say against other vested interests, whether less or more contrary to "public policy," or "sound principle," or any of those things he is accustomed to invoke in support of his evangel. But vested interest is not the vile and wicked thing which the reformer in his hurry and zeal deems it. It is only the right conferred on the individual by the laws and arrangements of society, of which the individual has taken lawful advantage. If the laws and arrangements were not the best that might have been, that was not the fault of the individual, and if he did nothing unlawful in the securing of the interest vested in him, it is scarcely for society to deprive him *ex post facto* of what it deliberately offered or intentionally conferred, and had bound itself by contract, express or implied, to confer. It is perhaps not going too far to say that no man can be righteously deprived of a gain, benefit, or advantage which he has by lawful means secured under existing laws and arrangements. His gain may be, almost certainly is, directly or indirectly another's loss; and though that other may grudge the gain, he cannot cancel it. In almost every contract for the sale of goods with delivery spread over a number of months, one of the parties has occasion to say that he could have done better by waiting; but that is not admitted as any reason for his resiling or breaking his contract. Hitherto the same has been the case in transactions with regard to land. The "unearned increment" doctrine is the first suggestion to change the law and practice and to make gain in land transactions of no advantage to the gainer. The advocates of the doctrine feel that there is an essential difference between land and chattels, and they are groping about for some means of marking and giving effect to the difference. They have not taken the right way.

Land is either a fit subject of private property, or it is not. If it is, then all the talk about unearned increment is so much nonsense. If it is not, then the reformer must face the task of showing how the error of our ancestors in making it private property is to be remedied without confiscation and injustice. British law has no favour for confiscation, and we pride ourselves as a people on our love of justice. We have seen that originally land is brought into cultivation only by those who claim to treat it as their own, and that, if the claim were not admitted, the land would probably be left without cultivation. If the claim must be admitted at one stage, we are entitled to ask the reformer to define the stage at which the ownership is to cease, or, on the occurrence of some defined event, the extent to which the property is to be taken from its *quondam* owner. The reformer has not had the courage to say that, on sound policy, land cannot be owned by the individual, and by allowing private ownership and claiming the unearned increment he has got into a quagmire of inconsistencies from which he has no chance of escape. The proposal to tax land values to an extent that would sweep away the increment, and the proposal to tax feu-duties, are proofs of the groping to which we have referred. They are expedients to accomplish that which no known principle would justify. They are unprincipled, though it has been attempted to justify them by principles framed for the occasion. These hand-to-mouth principles are in reform what the opportunist is in politics. Some are willing to use them, but nobody speaks well of them.

Chapter IX.

"PROPERTY" AND ITS LIMITATIONS.

THE essential difference which we have said the reformer sees (or feels) between land and chattels lies at the root of all land-law reform. We do not think the difference should be denied, or can be denied. I can live without my neighbour's millions, but I cannot live if I am denied all use of the land through the exercise of exclusive ownership and occupancy by others. The extinction of my neighbour's wealth might or might not affect me injuriously, but the extinction of the land would involve my extinction. Mismanage wealth, and it disappears. Manage or mismanage land, and it still remains. The difference between land and other kinds of property can hardly be denied; but how to recognise and give effect to the difference is the question which is the true land question.

We have already sought to establish that land is property, and that private ownership is both natural and necessary. We may now with advantage enquire what limits and conditions should be attached to private ownership. But, first, let us glance at the limits that have already been set to ownership in land. Though by the law of Scotland the owner claims everything from the heaven to the centre of the earth (*a centro usque ad coelum*), yet the Crown takes the gold and silver that may be found in the land. In times of peace the owner may build a wall round his property and keep out all the world, yet in times of war the Queen's army may pull his house about his ears if the commanding officer is of opinion that it would hinder his own movements or favour those of the enemy. If a railway is to be constructed (in the interest of the community, though at the immediate cost of the shareholders) the company can take compulsorily the land required for the line by paying its value, plus 50 per cent., whether the owner wishes or no. Moreover, no owner is at liberty by our law to use his own land to the detriment of his neighbour (*in emulatione vicini*). These examples of the limits set to private ownership in land lay the foundation in principle for further limitations which, we shall try to show, would meet the whole requirements of the case, if not the whole demand of the land-law reformer.

By the law of Scotland a land-owner has right to hold his land, to feu it or lease it on his own terms, and the still more remarkable right of neither using it himself nor allowing any one else to use it. If it contains minerals he may leave them in the bowels of the earth, and, though coal is at famine prices, he may refuse to let an ounce of his coal be brought to the surface. If he grant a feu he may insert in the charter a condition that no public-house shall be allowed in the buildings to be erected on the ground. He may thus pass a Local Option Bill without requiring the assent of Lords or Commons, and he may in this way exercise a higher power than the Licensing Court without his decision requiring confirmation. On such powers it might not be out of place to put some limit. When the land is made available for the wants of the community, and that on reasonable terms and conditions, land-law reform will have made great advance and the sore of the reformer will have been healed.

There is a natural tendency on the part of owners of all kinds of property to think they should be allowed to do what they please with their own. But this tendency, though natural, cannot in some cases be allowed full play. Public health forbids nuisance, and public wants impose taxes on land. Why should not public requirements or convenience force the owner to give off his land on reasonable terms? This would be the true remedy if the real evil is the holding of land for a rise in value, or the keeping it fallow when it is required for cultivation, or the holding it idle for policies or deer forests when it is wanted for the use of the community or any of its members. A limited ownership already exists and suggests further limitations to suit the circumstances of the times in which we live and the social conditions by which we are surrounded.

Let it be taken for granted, merely to save going through the argument by which it could be shown, that the absolute limit placed by nature on the extent of the land warrants our saying to its owners, "You may take all the profit you can get from your ownership, but you shall not so exercise that ownership as for a day or an hour to retard the progress of the community by hampering it or any of its members in the use of the land." Land-ownership cannot be tolerated if it is exercised by the owner for the time being in a spirit of obstruction, or selfishness, or otherwise than ownership would have to be exercised by an elected public body accountable for its stewardship to the community which elected it and had power to supersede it. On this principle land-ownership might imply profit, but would not confer absolute control. Such a limited ownership would not deprive land-owners of any realisable asset if the market value of the day had to be paid and accepted in every transaction forced on the owner. All that would in that case be taken away from the owner would be the power to hold his land for a rise in value to be produced through the action of the community, and the other still worse power to let it lie idle though members of the community are ready and willing to give its present value for the privilege of putting it to use. Present value and proper use of the land involve questions which could not be left to the owner and the first man who came forward claiming the use for payment of "present value." Provision would have to be made for settling these questions. Let us suggest the provisions.

Suppose that Lord Fielding owns 10,000 acres of land; that he has leased 8000 acres to farmers; that he holds 1000 acres in park policy and pasture land for the amenity of his mansion; and that the remaining 1000 acres are let meantime by the year as grass parks in the hope of feuing them at £20 per acre by and by. Little or nothing requires to be said about the 8000 acres; but what about the 1000 acres around the mansion house and the 1000 acres meant for feuing? Lord Fielding will naturally wish to keep his policies intact and to give off the feuing land in accordance with the feuing plan of the estate, which has been prepared with a view to secure and maintain the amenity of the mansion-house. If the land and its ownership existed for the benefit of Lord Fielding it would be necessary to give full effect to his lordship's wishes. But the land existed before Lord Fielding and was meant for mankind, though we are willing to give his lordship the full benefit of that limited ownership which the arrangements of our predecessors have conferred upon him. Let us now suppose that Mr. Mason comes forward and offers £10 (a year) of feu-duty for one acre of the feuing ground and £5 (a year) for one acre of the policies. The feuing ground, let as grass parks, is bringing in a rent of £4 per year per acre, and the policies, which are bringing in no rent, are entered by Lord Fielding on the valuation roll at £1 per acre. His lordship, if left to the freedom of his own will, would refuse both offers. He would refuse on any terms to feu the acre included in the policies, and he would ask £20 for the acre of his feuing ground. At once there are questions which the parties could never settle, and these questions would have to be referred to a tribunal of some sort.

Chapter X.

A LAND COURT AND ITS FUNCTIONS.

THE first question for the tribunal might be the suitability of Mr. Mason, and his right to come in as feuar to the exclusion of others. There might be competition for the ground, and of such competition the landowner should get the full benefit, according to our view of the matter. The Court would therefore require to make sure that Mr. Mason's offer is the best obtainable, and to afford the owner an opportunity to obtain a better offer, if a better is to be had. Now, let us suppose that Mr. Mason is the highest offerer for the feuing ground, but that his offer of £5 for the acre of the policies is outbid by that of £6 made by Mr. Slater. Lord Fielding is still unwilling to give off his feuing land at £10 an acre, and would not take £30 an acre for his policies if he could help it. The tribunal must now decide whether the use to which the two acres are proposed to be put is proper use. For this purpose Mason and Slater must declare and produce their plans, and after Lord Fielding's objections, if any, have been heard and considered, the Court would decide. As regards the feuing ground the only questions, after the value was ascertained, would be the suitability of the acre selected and of the buildings proposed to be erected upon it. The owner's interest in regard to the remainder of the ground would have to be kept in view on some such principles as regulate the feuing plans of superiors under the present *régime*.

But as regards the policies further considerations call for attention. It would be easy for Mr. Slater to select an acre in the park which, though no better for him, would be the most objectionable from the owner's standpoint. Though the owner, on grounds of public policy, may be compelled to give off land required for the purposes of the community, yet the claimant could not be allowed to use his powers capriciously, much less vindictively. He would therefore have to be restrained if in using his rights he sought to encroach unnecessarily on the amenity of the landowner's demesne, or to interfere unduly with the owner's feuing plan. The tribunal for settling these questions would therefore require to have power to deal with disputes about sites; and, as the *per contra* of compelling the land-owner to give off land which he would rather retain, the Court would require to have power to force the claimant, under a substantial penalty, to take the plot fixed by the Court as suitable for the purposes of the claimant. If the feuar thought fit to refuse the ground fixed by the Court, he might also be made liable for the whole cost of the proceedings which he had initiated.

If there were several competitors for the same piece of ground the land-owner would have no difficulty in *choosing* his feuar, especially if one offered more than the rest by way of feu-duty. It would not be consistent with what has gone before to deny the owner the benefit of competition, for competition would only bring out the market value of the ground in demand. But if the various competitors agreed as to the feuing value of the land, but did not agree to give way to one another as to special plots, it might be deemed contrary to public policy to allow the owner to prefer one of several offerers all offering the same feu-duty. Here again the Court would have to settle differences by selecting the offerer whose intended use of the ground should appear to be most for the good of the community. It is highly probable that offerers would try to settle the question for themselves by out-bidding one another in the feu-duty in order to put the land-owner in a position to give it to the highest bidder and prevent the delay and expense of a judgment by the Court. But as there might be cases where several persons offered the maximum feu-duty asked by the owner, and as favouritism would be contrary to the spirit of the law, provision must be made for disposing of conflicting but equal offers.

We may now glance at the question as to the land which a land-owner should be entitled to retain in his own hands without being bound to accept for it any rent or feu-duty, no matter how large. In the public interest land may be said to be properly used if it is under cultivation as farm land or pasture land, or is carrying such buildings, railways, canals, or other public works as the circumstances of the neighbourhood demand. Land is not properly used when it is retained to an undue extent for mere amenity, when it is held for deer forests though wanted for cultivation, when it is kept as farm land though required for buildings or public undertakings, or when it is allowed to lie idle for an expected rise in value as feuing ground or otherwise. All these improper uses retard the progress of the community. In all these cases, therefore, the owner should be compellable to give up his land for a proper use and for a proper consideration, *i.e.*, for market value. The average land-owner, especially the hereditary owner, and more especially the owner of entailed land, will of course see in all this a revolutionary interference with the sacred rights of property, from which, in his view, nothing but anarchy can be predicted. But others who are not land-owners, or whose mental vision is not distorted by self-interest, may fancy they see, on the contrary, a too liberal recognition of the rights of land-owners and a too generous appropriation to them of the profits arising from the action and enterprise of the community, *i.e.*, of third parties. Much, which it would serve no purpose to say here, might be said on both sides; but if we hold that land is a fit subject of private property and that the owner must hold his land subject to the public interest, it follows that the owner cannot be denied any part of the price obtainable for parting with it, and that when wanted in the public interest the land must be given off at its full current value. Let these two propositions be established and the skill of the parliamentary draughtsman will not be overtaxed in framing a Bill to give full and detailed effect to them in the form of a Land Act. The two great grievances under the present land-laws are (1) the owner's absolute power to hold his land idle and unproductive, and (2) his right to refuse all and every offer to put it to its natural and proper and necessary use. If these grievances were removed, the community would have all the advantages of free trade in land, land nationalisation, abolition of entail and primogeniture, and all the rest of it. These views, it will be observed, concede that we are bound by the arrangements of our ancestors, and that confiscation of existing realisable rights is not to be thought of. We do not go the length of thinking that the landowner has any moral right, on the strength of ancestral arrangements, to discount the needs of posterity, and to hold on to the land in the hope that a better buyer than the man of to-day may be looked for in the days to come. He may do that with his railway or insurance company shares, with his house and his horse, his furniture and his pictures, but not with his land, which is neither producing crops nor carrying houses.

Chapter XI.

NEED OF LAND COURT ILLUSTRATED.

IF this differentiation is questioned, just consider what would be the effect of refusal by all the landowners in the country to give off land, and of their determination to hold it idle, so far as not already leased or feued. There would be an end to the growth of towns and cities, trade would lose its expansiveness, national prosperity would come to its maximum, and, not being able to grow, would shrink, and an increase of population would be impossible from want of space on which to place it. The land-owners would, in the case supposed, exercise a power greater than that of Parliament, and that too without the necessity of framing, introducing, discussing, and passing any Bill, or asking any royal assent. Who would be a peer, or even a king, if he might be a land-owner with such vast powers! Now, suppose that all the shareholders of all the railway companies in the country were to refuse to sell their shares, nobody would be a half-penny the worse except the stockbrokers, who would lose their commissions, and the Exchequer, which would lose the stamp duty on transfers. A number of investors would be forced to look elsewhere for ways of putting their money out to interest, but the railways would be as useful as ever to the community. We may acknowledge, or we may deny, the difference between land and other kinds of property, but the difference remains. You may rescue land from the sea, but you cannot create a square yard of land beyond the limits set to it by Nature. The same thing is not true of any other kind of property. Though all kinds of what we call chattel property are obtained from the land, such property is capable of indefinite increase, though the land itself is not. You cut down a tree growing on the land, and you make it into furniture. You thereby use up and exhaust the tree, but the land is unchanged and capable of producing more trees. You may increase the productiveness of the land, but you cannot increase the land. That is the difference, and it both justifies and renders necessary different sets of rules for the regulation of things so different in their nature and attributes.

If all this is true, and if it has always been true, it is curious that society has so long allowed the "sacred" rights of private property in land to be carried so far, to the obstruction of the progress of society. The regard paid, and the respect shown, to private property, while necessary for the wellbeing, and even the existence, of society, have, in relation to land, redounded to the detriment of society. The explanation is perhaps to be found, not in the greed and domination of the landlord class (upon whom it has been the fashion to throw the whole blame), but in the failure by society itself to discriminate between land as property and other kinds of property with very different attributes. The failure to make distinctions where there are differences is the cause of confusion, and confusion of thought is the root of error, disorder, wrong, and injustice. It is unfair, but not surprising, that those who suffer the wrong and injustice should commit the further error of throwing the blame of it on the innocent shoulders of those who profit by it, but had no hand in bringing it about.

In times of famine, the people would tolerate no corner in wheat or any other food supply, and the government of the day have, in such times, fixed the price at which the bakers were bound to sell their loaves. In a certain sense there is always a famine of land, and the law might just as reasonably fix the price of land as, in times of famine, the price of bread. As soon as the famine is past, the holders of wheat are allowed to hold it or make it into bread as they may please, and, if they bake it, to charge the market price for the loaf. There is a famine of land whenever a member of the community has occasion for a piece of land to cultivate or build upon, which its owner is holding idle and unproductive merely from unwillingness to part with it, or in hope of a better price at a future date. The owner would suffer no wrong if the famine rule were applied to force him to take present value. If the wheat-holder, because the supply is short for the time being, may reasonably be forced to sell, much more the land-holder, whose commodity is always short and always diminishing as the community grows. Moreover, the wheat supply is rendered less valuable to its holder *as a means of personal sustenance* by any increase in the number of those who require to share it, while, on the contrary, the land has acquired all its saleable value from the growth of the community, against which the owner holds and wishes still to hold it. These distinctions are recognised in principle in the powers of compulsory purchase given, for instance, to railway companies and to local authorities in connection with sewage schemes, and in such proposed legislation as the Access to Mountains Bill. The next step, and it would not be a very long step, should be the conferring upon all and sundry a power of compulsory purchase on fair terms, and under proper supervision, of all land not in agricultural use or built upon, or devoted to some public or private purpose entitling it to be exempted from the operation of compulsory purchase.

Chapter XII.

THE TRIBUNAL.

The tribunal which has been suggested, and mentioned more than once, might be called the Land Court, and its powers might be the following, to begin with,—further powers being conferred as experience showed the need. The Court would determine whether the land brought into question was being put by its owner to such use as the public interest required. If in proper use, it would not be open to compulsory purchase; but if not in such use, its owner would be bound to feu it for a feu-duty equal to, say, 4 per cent. on its present capital value. We have already premised that the offerer has offered market value, and that his offer, if taken, would increase the income of the land-owner. The acceptance of the offer would put an end to the landowner's chances of larger gain from future increase in value; but that is the essence of the reform here brought under consideration. The next duty of the Court would be to find whether the lot chosen by the offerer was suitable in view of the land-owner's feuing plan, as well as the offerer's purposes. Then these purposes would have to be examined, and their suitability for the neighbourhood determined. The proposed buildings, if any, would also be taken into account, much as the Dean of Guild Court in Glasgow, for instance, supervises erections in that city. The fact that the price offered was the market value has been taken for granted; but if the land-owner disputed the price the Court, as we have said above, would give him an opportunity of showing that a better *bona fide* offer was obtainable. All these questions would be fought out under the ordinary rule as to costs, which would be a sufficient check against wrongful insistance on the part of the offerer or wrongful resistance on the part of the owner.

Many matters connected with the Land Court would require careful consideration. For instance, should it be fixed in Edinburgh, like the Court of Session, or scattered through the country, like the Sheriff Courts, or perambulatory, like the Crofters' Commission and the Circuit Court of Justiciary? What would be the proper qualification for the judge, and should there be one, or more than one, in each Court? If the duty were imposed on the Sheriff, would he hear skilled evidence, or have a practical assessor who would inspect the *locus*, and form his own opinion, to the exclusion of evidence by so-called experts? And from what branch of business would the assessor be drawn—land surveyors, architects, property valuators, builders, or what? As simplicity and economy would be chief aims under the new system, what costs would be allowed in the Land Court? and what form of procedure should be followed, written or oral, summary or ordinary, with right to call in the aid of lawyers, or only with their help when the Court gave its consent in difficult cases? As the amount involved, at least as an annual sum, would often be small, the whole arrangements connected with the Land Court would require to be as simple and inexpensive as possible. And in order not to confer too much power nor throw too much responsibility on the Court, the Act would require to contain elaborate definitions and rules, which would also tend to secure uniformity in the administration of the law throughout the country.

The effect of these changes would be far-reaching. They would amount to a practical abolition of the law of entail, so far as the public is concerned. The income from the land might remain under the fetters of the entail, but the land itself would be freed, which is the point of public interest. The law of primogeniture would lose its feature offensive to the public, for, though the whole landed estate might go as heretofore to the eldest son, that would not hinder the appropriation of the land to any lawful or desirable purpose. The holding up of land for a rise would cease when every land-owner was bound to sell at market value. The remedy we propose for the evils of our ancient land system is perhaps too simple to commend itself to the minds of ardent reformers. Those who cling to "time-honoured" institutions may object to our proposal on the ground that it is not in harmony with the feudal system. The obvious answer to these objectors is that the feudal system is not in harmony with the times, and as we cannot adjust the times to the feudal system, and as that system has served its day—and more—we can afford to part with it, and nobody will be a penny the worse.

Chapter XIII.

TITLE-DEEDS AND CERTIFICATES OF TITLE.

If the feudal system were abolished *de jure* as well as *de facto* it would be much easier than it is now to open the door for the simplification of titles, in the sense of title-deeds. By the Scottish system of Land Registers a man's right is complete only as far as it has found its way to the Register of Sasines. A right higher than that shown by the Register, or a right which has not reached the Register at all, may belong to a man, but it is imperfect till it appears on the records. A search of the records is accepted by conveyancers as evidence of the state of the title, but only in the negative sense that there are no rights except those disclosed by the search. For positive evidence the title-deeds themselves, or official extracts of recorded deeds, must be forthcoming. Surely an official copy or extract or certificate of what the Register contains would be as good as the parcel of writs of which the certificate could quite easily give the result. No matter what right to, or in relation to, land a man may hold, his title-deeds show it. They do not constitute the right, they are merely evidence of it. Thus, title-deeds, though commonly regarded as documents of title, are more strictly evidences of title, and they are so recognised in the phrase "writs and evidents." When a conveyancer draws, engrosses, and records a deed constituting or transmitting a land right he is not so much constituting or transmitting the right as providing evidence that the right had, by antecedent contract, or succession, been already constituted or transmitted. This is very plainly so in the case, for example, of a Notarial Instrument, by the expeding and recording of which testamentary trustees make up their title to a property conveyed to them in the trust settlement, under the comprehensive "All and sundry the whole means and estate heritable and moveable which shall belong to me at the time of my decease." The right of the trustees dates from the moment of the testator's death. The Notarial Instrument is only the form of evidence which our feudal law and registration system demand in proof of the right and of its completion. It is, in the language of the feudal system, made "real" by the recording of the Notarial Instrument, but the right existed from the testator's death while the Instrument was yet unwritten.

What the conveyancer, the antiquary, and those whose reverence for the past is greater than their faith in the future would call a serious departure from the principles of the feudal system might, after all, be nothing more than an alteration in the law of evidence. For instance, we think a certificate by the keeper of the Register of Sasines, describing the property and, in the fewest possible words, stating the right which the owner holds therein, and the qualifications thereto, if any, would be a much more convenient title-deed than conveyancers find in the "progress," as they call the parcel of writs through which they have to wade for their information under our present system. Any right is found capable of definition and description when it is sold, and when the buyer's agent is drawing the conveyance for transmitting it. We need not doubt, therefore, that the keeper of the Register could as easily define and describe the right in his certificate. If the whole right were sold, what is to hinder the seller to hand his certificate, endorsed, to the buyer, and so to transmit to the buyer the whole right, title, and interest of the seller? And if the buyer produce the endorsed certificate to the keeper of the record, what is to hinder the keeper from entering the endorsation in the record, and thereby divesting the seller, and completing the investiture of the buyer? And if only a part of the owner's right were sold, two new certificates could be issued—one for the right reserved, and one for the right sold; and the old certificate could be destroyed, or returned for preservation meantime, and cancellation at the end of a fixed time. In the case of *pro indiviso* ownership, a certificate might be granted for delivery to the first-named of the owners, and the others could have duplicate certificates. In cases of succession the heir, on establishing his right, could have his ancestor's certificate endorsed to him by the Court, and if there were more heirs than one, the first-named heir could have the certificate, and each of the others could have a duplicate. In all these cases the registration of the endorsement would complete the title; and in none of these suggestions is there proposed any change except a change in the law of evidence, as applied to land rights.

Chapter XIV.

THE REFORMER AND HIS OBSTACLES.

Our education in the feudal system has fostered in us the belief that a right to, or connected with, land could not safely be treated like any other right of property. Perhaps the system of land rights and writs that has come down to us was perfectly, or only imperfectly, suited to our ancestors, who created the system, but most thoughtful men are agreed that it has outlived its day, and "lags superfluous on the stage." The public have no doubt at all that the expense of transferring land is monstrous, but as each buyer is less anxious to reform the law than to be made safe, he grumbles at the cost and conforms to the practice. He has no time just then to look after a reform of the law; and even if he had, he does not understand it well enough to know how and where to begin. And so the system lasts and becomes more venerable year by year. The utmost that the official reformer (*i.e.*, the reformer who is an official) usually attempts is to cut and carve at the form and length of the writs of conveyancing, and on great occasions, and as an exhibition of extra courage, to lop off a writ altogether, but saving always the feudal system in its "principles," as they are called. He does all this well knowing that the essential principles of the feudal system as understood fifty years ago are dead and gone. But the system is not abolished from a sort of cowardly fear that some unknown evils would arise if the system were not kept lying, as it were, on the shelf, to be brought down, on the emergence of those evils, to cure and conquer them by its principles, and the virtue contained in them. What appears to be wanted is a man who understands the feudal system, and knows it is dead, and does not wish to keep its corpse above ground, but would bury it decently, and then sit down and frame a new system suited to the times and its requirements in the matter of simplicity and economy. With proper clerical assistance he could do the work in a year, though it might take him ten years to answer the objections that would come from all sorts of quarters.

But the "man who understands the feudal system and knows it is dead," if he did not happen to be a Lord Advocate, would have it hinted to him, less or more plainly, that he was not supposed to know how to deal with legal reform and had better leave it to those who do know, to wit, the responsible legal advisers of the Crown. Now, these gentlemen have their official and parliamentary duties to perform and, what is worse, they have their party to consider, so they have no time, and perhaps less inclination, to undertake in their official character what others, who may be willing and able, may not do from want of official position. The present writer went into this difficulty somewhat fully in an article entitled "Wanted an Officer" which appeared in the pages of the *Scottish Law Review* for October, 1891 (vol. vii. p. 293), to which the reader, if he is interested in the matter, is referred. No matter how competent the man may be who ventures to bring forward a measure of reform of the land laws, he is certain to encounter the official cold-shoulder and to suffer all its consequences. Let it not be supposed that these consequences are trifling, for they are very serious and obstructive. The world bows down to officialdom, and attaches more value to the opinion of mediocrity in office than it puts on the opinion of a man who is not in office, no matter how worthy of respect his views may be. As the law officers of the Crown are appointed and paid for administering the existing law, and have no mandate or contract to reform the law, it would be a great public gain if it were to be clearly established that law reform must come from any quarter rather than the official. A measure of reform would then have some chance of being looked at on its merits instead of being bowed out by official jealousy or made to give place to a Bill of his own which the Lord Advocate of the day is about to bring in, but doesn't, or, if he does, allows to drop to make way for some party measure. The men best qualified to deal with the reform of the land laws are the practising conveyancers of Scotland if they took up the subject with a due regard to the interests of the public, and a due disregard of their own interests from the selfish and narrow standpoint.

Opposition to reform would come from the landowners, but, as they are in the main reasonable and patriotic, they would not stand much or long in the way. Their interests would seem to be threatened, but their rights would be saved, and when there is no confiscation the landowner is not troublesome. It is not confiscation to have to take the market value, though it would be an interference with that freedom of contract which landowners have so long enjoyed, and some of them have so often abused. But the freedom of contract would not be lost: it would only be transferred to the landless or those wanting land. The transference would be made on the principle that if land is a good thing it should be divided, and monopoly in it abolished. The most violent opposition to the reform we have suggested would come from the thorough-going reformer, the man who proceeds on principle, the man who hates half-measures. Having made up his mind that land is not a fit subject of private property, or that the unearned increment belongs to the public, he can be satisfied with nothing but an immediate readjustment which would put matters where they would have been if his views had been acted on by his remote ancestors and all their successors. This opponent would be like a child crying for the moon. Like the child who stops crying for the moon when that luminary disappears, this opponent would probably come to reason when the rest of the people accepted the reform as a fair solution of the question. Officials connected with the Registers might also have to be dealt with, but as no one expects reform suggestions from them no one would be much influenced by their objections. Even the Exchequer might take alarm and oppose conveyance by endorsement through fear of losing the duties at present payable on conveyances. A bill or promissory note for £1000 on a 10s. stamp may be endorsed as often as you please without payment of further stamp duty, but though the duty on a conveyance of land worth £1000 is £5, it must be paid as often as the property changes hands. And yet people talk as if it were only lawyers who made land transfer costly. Conveyance by endorsement would get rid of the *ad valorem* fees of conveyancers, and when a Liberal Chancellor of the Exchequer gets a Liberal Government to take off the stamp duty on conveyances by endorsement, land transfer will have been made cheap and easy, and a grievance of long standing will have been ended. When will this happen, and will it ever happen? It passes the wit of man to say, just yet. The reform mill grinds so slowly.

Chapter XV.

OTHER OBSTACLES TO REFORM.

To secure the acquiescence of the Inland Revenue department (*i.e.*, of the Chancellor of the Exchequer) in the proposed reform it might be necessary to submit to the same duty on endorsements as, under the present rules, we pay on Conveyances. That is not a matter of principle, and we need not pursue it beyond saying that, if the duty were remitted and the State requirements could not spare the sum obtained from the duty, it would be put on something else. We should then see whether the desire for cheapening the transfer of land would reconcile the public to a transference of the tax to anything else. It is also a matter of detail, and not of principle, whether the endorsement should be merely recorded in the Land Register and the endorsed deed retained by the endorsee, or whether the endorsed deed should be given up to the Registrar and a new deed issued in favour of the endorsee. A bill of exchange passed by endorsation is a precedent for the one course, and a transfer of railway stock handed in with the old certificate and exchanged for a new certificate would be a precedent for the other plan. Either would be good enough; but the first would be easier and cheaper, while the second would be clearer.

Even amongst lawyers, moreover lawyers who claim to be reformers, there is a common taking-it-for-granted sort of belief that the various and complex rights with which they are familiar in relation to land could not be transmitted and vouched in the simple fashion which is here proposed. The objection was stated in the following words in a recent newspaper article on conveyancing reform: "*We must abandon the hope that we shall be able to make the transfer of, it may be, an irregular-shaped tenement in the heart of a busy city, with its conditions as to lights, and obligations as to common closes or washing-houses, and maintenance of roads, foot-paths, and drains, as simple as the transfer of a square mile of land in the backwoods of America.*" The writer of the words here quoted had not taken the trouble to look about for a way out of the difficulty, for if he had looked he would soon have found the way, or some way. Whatever the right of the owner may be, it is defined in the title-deeds, with all its conditions, provisions, reservations, and so on. Perhaps no one deed contains the whole, for in the later deeds the conditions, &c., may be only referred to as contained in some earlier deed or deeds entered in the Register. There is nothing to hinder a conveyancer from setting forth in one document both the nature of the right and its whole qualifications, as indeed he does when, on a purchase by his client, he makes "notes" on the progress of titles offered to him by the seller. One document drawn up in suitable form would be a convenient title-deed for the holder of the right, and much more convenient than the twenty, thirty, forty, or fifty writs which at present go to make up his title, and require to be examined at every transmission.

Chapter XVI.

THE CERTIFICATE OF TITLE.

THE form of document which *per se* would be a suitable and convenient certificate of ownership might be made so elastic as to serve for any and every sort of right in connection with land. Let us assume that the new Land Act fixed a day on which the present Registers of Sasines were to close, and that it also ordained the keepers of these registers to issue to all applicants certificates of ownership in exact conformity with the registers as on the appointed day. There would be time before the appointed day for owners to see that their rights had been duly entered in the registers, and to supply any defects of registration that might be found. After the appointed day an owner would apply for his certificate of ownership, and send in, along with his application, his title-deeds and an abstract showing the particulars of the right which the certificate should contain. These documents would be examined in conjunction with the registers, and the abstract would be found to be either correct or incorrect. If found to be incorrect, the keeper and the applicant would have to correct the error; and when the abstract was found to be correct, either as first sent

THE CERTIFICATE OF TITLE. 71

in or after correction, the keeper would issue his certificate perhaps in some such form as the following :—

On 1st January, 1900,
John Thomson, Druggist, 10 Princes St., Edinburgh,
is the owner of
The piece of ground measuring 1000 square yards on the south side of Sauchiehall Street, Glasgow, and bounded on the north by Sauchiehall Street, along which it extends   feet; on the east by ground belonging to A B, along which it extends   feet; on the south by ground belonging to C D, along which it extends   feet; and on the west by ground belonging to E F, along which it extends   feet.

Conditions and Burdens :—(e.g.).

Buildings to be stone and slated, not more than three storeys in height; and fronts to be of polished ashlar.

Prohibition against buildings being used otherwise than as dwelling-houses.

Obligation to asphalte pavement or lay it down with Caithness flagstones.

Feu-duty, £1 10s.

Ground-annual, £75; with duplication every 19th year from Whitsunday, 1890.

Bond for £2000 at 5 per cent. interest.

G. H.,
Keeper of the Land Register.

Land Registry, Edinburgh,
　1st July, 1900.

The variations on the above form of certificate would necessarily be very numerous, and amplification would often be required. But as there is nothing which a search would not discover, the keeper would have no great trouble in framing his certificate. Indeed, the abstract given in by the owner might be the work of a notary public who should be held responsible for its accuracy, just as at present he is answerable for notarial instruments expede by him.

With his certificate in his hand the owner could sell his right and deliver a good and unimpeachable title by endorsing on the certificate before handing it over:—

Sold as on 15th May, 1901,
To Peter Watson, Stationer, 35 Union St., Glasgow,
At the price of £3000.

John Thomson.

Mr Watson would present the endorsed certificate at the Land Registry, and at same time pay the stamp duty (if any) due on the sale, as also the price of a new certificate which in due course the keeper would deliver. Or it might be optional for the buyer's agent to draw up the new certificate and to send it to the keeper with the endorsed certificate, and the keeper might be bound to sign the new certificate and to return it within a short period for a smaller fee than he would charge if he had to frame the new certificate.

Now, suppose the owner sells only part of his

property, or right, the endorsement would have to show what was sold, and two new certificates would have to be issued—one to the seller for the thing retained, and one to the buyer for the thing sold.

The Land Register might be kept on the principle of a ledger in which each separate right would have its own page, and on this page each transaction with regard to that right would be entered. In order to render searches unnecessary the buyer would defer payment of the price until, on presentation of the seller's certificate endorsed by the seller in his favour, the keeper of the Land Register had passed the endorsation as not forbidden by either inhibition or adjudication. The keeper would keep or have access to the Inhibition Register, and it could be made part of his duty to see whether the seller is inhibited, and to certify that he is or that he is not. The creditor or other party obtaining decree of adjudication could be held bound, under pain of nullity of his decree, to have it entered in the Land Register. Until the decree was entered in the Register the *nexus* would not exist and the owner would be free to sell.

The certificate of title has been looked at with reference to the *transmission* of land rights, but it could easily be adapted to the *constitution* of these rights, both rights of property and rights of security. Suppose a landowner is feuing an acre of land, what is to hinder his law agent, instead of drawing up a feu contract according to the present form and practice, to fill up a certificate of title with all the particulars of the grant? The land-owner could sign the certificate (which he would understand much better than he understands the present feu contract), and it could then be sent to the Land Register to be recorded and signed by the keeper, and so rendered sufficient as a certificate of title. It would thus serve the double purpose of a feu contract (or deed of constitution) and of a certificate of title.

It would be the duty of the Registrar to open, as we might say, a new ledger account in the Land Register for the acre of land feued as a new right constituted, and also to enter the feu right on the page containing the land-owner's entry. Similarly, the lender of money on the security of land might obtain from the borrower a certificate of title as owner in security and could proceed to put his right on the register in the same way as the feuar. In the case of the bondholder, it might be made unnecessary to encumber the certificate of title with more than the description or definition of the land burdened, the date and amount of the loan, and the rate of interest. Such deeds of constitution and certificates of title combined could be transferred by endorsation as already explained with regard to certificates of title to be issued to owners standing on the records on the day appointed for the commencement of the new system.

We have still to see how far the certificate of title would be suited to the transmission of land rights from the dead to the living, and to the extinction of such rights. Take extinction first. The extinction of any right in land, except the right of security, is so uncommon that we need not, here at least, extend our view beyond security rights. Resignations *ad perpetuam remanentiam* were feudal expedients more frequently than mercantile transactions. The holder of the security, when he receives payment either in full from the debtor or in part from the realization of the security, could endorse his certificate of title thus :—

1st July, 1901.

Received payment in full

[or *Received payment of £950 from the sale of the property, leaving a balance of £50 unpaid*]

(Signature)

The surrender of the certificate and the registration of the endorsement would disburden the subject of security. If the creditor desired to preserve recourse for the unpaid balance, the endorsed certificate could be got back from the Land Register marked by the keeper :—

Valid only as a voucher of debt for £50 due by A B.

G. H.,

Keeper of the Land Register.

(Date)

Now, take transmission from the dead to the living. It is of two kinds: by conveyance *mortis causa* and by inheritance *ex lege*. The disponee of the conveyance (whether in property or in trust) would produce the conveyance and the disponer's certificate of title, and the heir to the inheritance would produce his service and his ancestor's certificate of title. In exchange for the certificate and exhibition of the conveyance (if, containing more, it could not be delivered), the disponee would get a new certificate, while the heir would have to deliver his ancestor's certificate plus the service in order to obtain his new certificate.

In what goes before it has been taken for granted that the certificate of title, whether issued on the constitution or on any subsequent transmission of a right, would contain every condition and burden affecting the property. In many cases this would be simple and convenient, but in other cases it would not. It would not suit where the conditions are as voluminous as, for instance, in a deed of entail. A too elaborate certificate would expose the new system to the reproach of being as bad, and would tend to make it as costly, as the old. For cases where the conditions are lengthy the plan might be adopted of making the original writ by the disponer (*i.e.*, the certificate of title of the original disponee) do duty as showing the permanent burdens and of attaching to it (on the same or on separate paper) the certificate of title of subsequent owners. A distinction might be made between burdens and conditions in their nature permanent, such as the feu-duty, and burdens in their nature temporary, such as a bond for borrowed money, The certificate of title in force at the moment would have to show, by detailed statement, or by reference to certificate attached containing such statement, all existing burdens, but a discharged burden, such as a bond after it had been paid up, need no longer be noticed. Temporary burdens might therefore be kept off the certificate of permanent burdens and inserted in the latest certificate, if there were two in use.

Such an indication in outline as we have given may appear to the careless reader as shadowing forth a system as complicated as that with which it is brought into competition. That, however, is what only the careless reader would say. Any one who takes the trouble to think out the matter and follow the suggestions with sufficient care to make him familiar with them will discover that on each transmission very much less would require to be done than at present, and very much less paid for the doing of it. Take, for illustration, a simple case of transmission on sale of a tenement fifty years old at a price of £3000 burdened with a bond for £2000. The seller would produce, let us say, two certificates, connected by letter and number, as his whole title. The older certificate would contain the full description of the ground and all the conditions of the feu. The second certificate would show who is the present owner and the bond for £2000. The buyer's agent would present both certificates at the Land Register, and the keeper would certify that they agreed with the Register and that there was no inhibition or adjudication against the seller or property. The buyer would then pay his £1000, and get a new certificate in exchange for the seller's second certificate. The first or older certificate would be handed to the buyer, whose title would be completed without more ado. Of course the keeper of the Land Register would do his part by entering the buyer on the Register as now the owner. The two certificates being connected by the reference letter and number, the whole thing would in time become so simple that buyers and sellers would find courage to dispense with the services of lawyers. After that the millennium! A guinea for the lawyer, if one was employed, and half a guinea for the keeper of the Land Register, would pay for all the work they would have to do; and if £1 11s. 6d. was thought too much, the guinea could be saved and the cost kept down to 10s. 6d. By comparison with the present expenses, this would surely be thought a cheapening of the cost of land transfer.

Chapter XVII.

MINOR POINTS OF REFORM.

If the plan we have suggested were described with fulness in all its details, the broad features would be hidden in the mass of particulars. On the other hand, an outline such as we have given exposes the scheme perhaps to the taunt of not being worked out as a scheme must be which is to be of any use in practice. To this we reply that objections can be brought forward and discussed on the outline just as easily as on the most detailed exhibition of the new system; and that it is the business of the parliamentary draughtsman, rather than the reformer, to work out the details after the scheme has been approved of in its main features. Intelligent readers will therefore make due and reasonable allowance for want of elaboration of the system recommended, while they will have no difficulty in forming an opinion on the system itself. In passing, however, we may observe that the certificate of title and plan of Land Register could easily be adapted to deal with destinations in liferent and fee, or the destinations to be found in deeds of entail. The destination would be added after the name of the owner, but only if it called heirs or successors other than those whom the law would nominate. There would be no need then (there is only a conform-to-practice need now) to write a destination in favour of "heirs and assignees whomsoever, heritably and irredeemably." Anything else than this is not to be presumed, so this should not require to be stated.

Our new system does not involve any change in the law of succession, nor (of necessity) in the manner of finding judicially who is the heir to the dead owner. Something much less elaborate than the present proceedings in special and general services might, however, be devised without danger to the patrimonial interests of anybody. What is to hinder the Sheriff of the county to take the evidence of two witnesses to prove the propinquity, and to write at the end of the proof "I find that A is the heir of B"? and, without troubling the Sheriff of Chancery or anyone else, why should not A produce this finding and B's certificate of title, and get from the Land Register a new certificate in his own name? The land-law reformer always demands the abolition of entail and primogeniture, but if the system of land rights which we advocate were adopted the public would have no concern with these feudal expedients for preventing the partition of landed estates. Compel the owner of the day to accept the price of the day for his land, and the public has no concern with the owner's arrangements for sending on his remaining rights to his successors. The only effect of entail seems to be the keeping of property in the wrong hands, and the thwarting of the law of "the survival of the fittest." No doubt it gratifies in some measure the feeling of "family pride," but observation teaches us that, however natural it may be to be proud of one's progenitors, it is risky to show pride, in advance, in one's progeny. But if land were held subject to compulsory sale at current prices it would not concern the public whether a landower left his estates under entail to a selected series of heirs, or to one heir or a dozen heirs. If the land as an article of commerce were relieved, as our reform would relieve it, from the fetters of entails, it would not matter whether the income from the land were concentrated in one heir or divided amongst all the heirs possessed of equal natural claims. Public policy might have something to say, but the land-law reformer, as such, would not be concerned.

Under the feudal system the man who has right to a feu-duty (of any amount) from a plot of ground is grandiloquently called the superior, and is said to hold the *dominium directum* of the ground, while the man who is the true owner of the plot and pays the feu-duty is called the vassal and is said to hold the *dominum utile*. The so-called superior is in effect nothing more than a first bondholder for a sum which he cannot call up, and of which the annual interest is the amount of the feu-duty. For failure for two years to pay the feu-duty his remedy is resumption of the ground—in feudal language, irritancy of the feu.

Under any new system of land rights, is anything to be gained by treating the so-called superior as anything else than a preferred creditor or first bondholder? He has sold, or been forced to sell, his ground at the price of, say, £20 a year, to be paid in perpetuity. Is anything to be lost by saying that his right to the land is given away for an annuity, and that he can take back the land if the annuity is not paid for two years? Practically, the resumption of the feu for non-payment is unknown, because the buildings erected by the feuar, which would go back to the man who gave off the vacant ground, make it worth the while of the feuar, or failing him the bondholder, to pay the feu-duty even when the buildings are bringing in no revenue. Thus the superior's remedy of irritancy is a sort of feudal curiosity of which the student of conveyancing hears much and the conveyancer sees nothing. It might therefore be judicious to make the certificate of title of the quondam superior a certificate of a burden of £20 of feu-duty payable from the lands described in the certificate. A proper preference could be given by the Act of Parliament to feu-duties over first and and all other bonds affecting the ground. In other words, why not abolish as a theory what has long since lost its significance in fact, and be done with terminology like superior and vassal, entry and non-entry, infeft and uninfeft, casualty and composition, and all the rest of it? Nothing survives of the feudal system except its "superior" exactions and its theories,—the former for the benefit of land owners, and the latter for obstructing the simplification of land transfer. "Nothing survives" is perhaps too strong a phrase, in view of the fact that a superior can still arrogate to himself the functions of the Sheriffs of the county and of Chancery combined, by granting a writ of clare constat making A (or rather declaring A to be) the heir of B in the lands held by B "of and under" the superior. Moreover, the superior may exercise this judicial function if only "it clearly appear" to him that A is the heir of B though no proof be led to establish the fact. What a fuss the poor Sheriffs must make before they venture to "find" what at least two witnesses must have testified, that A is the heir of B. Notwithstanding writs of clare constat and a few other odds and ends of feudal antiquity, the system is dead; but its friends don't like to mention the fact, and so it remains above ground.

Chapter XVIII.

GENERAL CONSIDERATIONS.

THE lovers of antiquity who reverence the past, the feudal conveyancers, and those who say: "rather bear those ills we have than fly to others that we know not of" will unite in condemning the vandalism of our suggestions, and will talk of the sacrilege of "so-called reformers," and may even revive that useful quotation —"fools rush in where angels fear to tread." They may not mention who are the fools, but they will leave no doubt who are the angels. These angels, however, are a sort that do not leave the world much better than they found it. In the great struggle for existence (of which "superior" people as a class know less than most others) it is thought (by those who think) that every obstacle in the way of the struggler should be removed. Unnecessary formalities and preventible expense, both of which adhere so tenaciously to the transfer of land, are obstacles which every reformer who has looked at our subject concurs in condemning. But as all proposals for improvement in these respects have hitherto been coupled with others involving confiscation, the reformer has called up hosts of defenders of the *status quo* in its entirety who would not have any interest or inclination to oppose a reform which saved their patrimonial rights. It is all very well to inveigh against vested interests, but we will look in vain for a class ready to stand by and witness in silence the destruction of their rights or even the curtailment of their privileges. Reformers must therefore, like every one else, take human nature as they find it. A measure of selfishness is both lawful and necessary for the very existence of man. This constant quantity in human character has its noble limitations and also its ignoble extensions. If we admire Boaz for taking care that Ruth should find it worth her while to glean in his fields, what shall we say of the artist who draws on the generosity of the public by drawing his pictures on the pavement, and, when the daylight fades, rubs out his daubs lest anyone else should, by means of them, obtain a share of that same generosity? Seeing such contrasts in human character, need we wonder at any defence of vested right or privilege sanctioned by law or usage? If the maintenance of the right or exercise of the privilege involve no injustice to others, the reformer must leave them alone, but if they unfairly hinder others in the race of life, the right becomes a wrong and the privilege becomes an injustice.

Unless we propose to cancel the past, to undo all that our ancestors did, to unmake all social arrangements, and to slip out of all contracts by which we are not the gainers, society must, in our opinion, take land-holding in the sense of land-owning as it has come down to us. Land has its present value to its owners, and it would be confiscation and injustice to take away any part of that value even on public grounds and for the public behoof. There would be no injustice to land-owners in a universal strike by the public against the doing of anything which would raise the value of the land to the land-owners. If it were possible for the public to leave the land-owners as sole occupiers of the land for even one year, very little imagination will enable us to picture the misery of the unhappy owners. The wail from Caledonia would be like the cry from Macedonia,—" Come over and help us." At the end of the year, whoever might doubt the source of land values, the land-owners would not. As an inducement to come, the public would be allowed to make their own terms. These would be less favourable to the owners than the terms we have proposed, so we may, may we not? take credit for being liberal to the land-owner. By our plan he would simply be forbidden, in one view to obstruct progress, in another view to levy toll on progress. He could not call either of these a hardship unless he first showed that he holds what lawyers call a "lien" on human effort to improve the condition of the race. Before we take anything from the land-owners which they at present possess, we must perhaps show our zeal for the public and the taxpayer by refusing payment of perpetual pensions bestowed before our own day. So long as we hold ourselves bound by gratuitous obligations voluntarily undertaken by our ancestors, but not terminable with the generation who gave them, we are surely bound to respect land rights, most of which are now held by purchasers or their heirs, though some few may still be held by the heirs of donees who gave no value for the grants they obtained.

Chapter XIX.

TAXATION OF LAND.

THE Land Question has so many ramifications that we despair, on the one hand, of exhausting the subject, and must plead guilty, on the other hand, to the introducing of matters which may seem apart from the subject. But as the land is the only thing we have to go on for position, profit, or pleasure, there is hardly anything the Land Question does not touch. We may now look at the taxation of land and of income from land. By income from land we mean what is paid for sheer land as distinguished from rent of buildings. Both alike are liable to the Imperial Exchequer for property or income tax; but while rents pay local taxes, feu-duties don't. Rents of grass parks and rents of shootings pay local taxes. A curiosity of our tax system is this: if a landowner draw an income of £6 for two acres of land let as grass parks, the £6 swells the assessable rental of the parish; but if he feu off the two acres at £10 an acre, the £20 is exempt from local rates. If the feuar build houses on the two acres to yield a rental of £1000, the whole £1000 is liable for local rates. Solomon, speaking of things which transcended his wisdom, said, "There be three things which are too wonderful for me, yea, four which I know not." If he had lived in our day he would have made the figure five, after studying our system of taxing. B invests his money in building houses, while A invests his in the purchase of feu-duties. When the local tax-gatherer sends out his demand notes, "A is happy; B is not"—to quote a line from a popular poet. The explanation of the difference is not wanting, but is it satisfactory? The man who draws an income from land in the name of feu-duty has parted with the control of the land to the feuar, and has, as we saw above, nothing more than a first bond over the land for a sum, of which the feu-duty is the interest. The interest on other bonds coming after this first bond is not taxed for local purposes. If you tax one, you must tax all bonds; and if you did, lenders would stipulate for relief by borrowers from local taxation in addition to the interest on the loan. The feuar who did not need to borrow would pay taxes once, while the feuar who had to borrow would pay taxes twice. The result would not be "equal," for the poor feuar would suffer, while the monied feuar would escape. On the principle that the consumer of a commodity must pay all costs of production and transport, and all profits from the maker to the retailer inclusive, may we not be sure that the occupier of a house or shop will be made to pay all the burdens laid on the capital represented by the premises?

The system by which in this country the money is raised for imperial and local purposes is so complex as to put it beyond the knowledge of those who bear the burden. The army of taxmen is vast, and they increase the burden of the taxes. It might, or it might not, be consistent with our present land laws, but it would be in keeping with the system of rights outlined above, to throw the whole taxes of the country upon the land. Imagine the community relieved of all taxes, direct and indirect—customs, excise, inland revenue (including stamps, death duties, and legacy and succession duty), and burgh, county, and parish rates—and in place of them all conceive a single tax on the basis of the valuation roll of the whole area of the country. Several results would follow. Tens of thousands of taxmen would become producers, instead of mere consumers of what others produce. There would be no chance of cheating the revenue. It would be known with almost absolute accuracy how much the tax would bring in, and the cost of collection would be reduced to the lowest point. Suppose that 1s. per £ were wanted, it might be imposed on the annual value or rent of the land and of everything upon it and minerals taken out of it, as at present, and also on all income from land, such as feu-duty and ground annuals, but not on interest on bonds, which are not permanent burdens on land. In this way ownership would pay all the taxes, and it might be safely left to the parties interested to adjust the incidence between owner and occupier. The matter would adjust itself if freed from the curse of artificiality and complexity which has hitherto followed it. A good deal on principle could be said in favour of exempting buildings, for the reason that they are not permanent while the land is a constant quantity. But as the owner of buildings (which enhance land values) is also an owner (even if a limited owner) of the land on which they stand, his ownership of the land makes him liable, if we adopt the principle that those who own the country should pay its taxes. If they retain the land in their own hands, they must pay, and if they give it off for a return in money, they will make that return recoup them for the tax. No matter how high the tax might run per £, the community would pay less than at present by reason (without counting others) of the saving of salaries to whole armies of officials who would no longer be wanted.

But the greatest result of all would be unification and simplification. The simplification needs no vindication, and the unification would be consistent with the broadest sense of the word "community." The interdependence of town and country, city and city, would be recognised, and the parochial notion would be exploded under which one parish pays a poor rate of 5s. per £ while another parish escapes for 6d. per £. It would be felt that the poor are the nation's poor, not the poor of the parish, and an end would be put to the unworthy and degrading efforts of one parish to throw the cost of a pauper on some other parish, or to send him back to his parish of origin.

The unification of taxes at the present time is Utopian or at least millennial, and may be dismissed with a mere mention in the way of honourable mention. If our heads cannot touch the stars, that is no reason why we should not admire constellations through a telescope. If taxes were unified all at once and in our day, what a scramble there would be for the biggest share out of the common fund! The town would grudge the country the cost of roads "leading to nowhere," and the country would object to the public money being spent on parks, and especially on music in the parks. The battle of appropriation and apportionment would scarcely be less bitter than the present quarrel as to incidence. The abolition of all taxes except a tax on the land, so arranged as to take most from those who gain most from it, may be only an idle dream, but it is a pleasant dream. Even in dreams thoughts sometimes come which are useful in real life. We do not say that simplification of taxes could be carried the length of unification, but the highest aim at simplification is needed to achieve even moderate improvement on our growingly complex and all but unworkable system of raising the money wanted for our ever-increasing public purposes. This is not the place to elaborate a taxation reform, and whether the land should bear the whole burden or less or more (than at present) of the burden must be left to others to discuss and settle.

CHAPTER XX.

MINERALS.

MINERALS cannot be left out of view in a discussion of the Land Question. They have received a full share of the land-reformer's attention, but hitherto without result. Under existing law the minerals go with the surface; and in what has gone before as regards the surface we have not favoured anything that savours of confiscation. But as we have not hesitated to advocate compulsory disposal of the land, neither shall we shrink from maintaining that the minerals may be taken out on equitable conditions, whether the land-owner consents or not. The cases in which the surface is owned by one and the minerals by another are so uncommon and exceptional as to make it unnecessary in our consideration of this branch of the subject to distinguish these cases from the ordinary case of ownership of the surface and all below it—*a centro usque ad coelum.* The great difference between land and minerals is that, by use, the minerals are exhausted, while the surface is not. No matter what income an owner may obtain from the surface, he leaves the surface for others; but if he work out, or, for a royalty, allow others to work out the minerals, he exhausts them. To put the matter in a homely way, he takes a greater liberty with the minerals than with the surface. Society can less afford his treatment of the minerals than his use of the surface. Whatever may have been the case in former times, it is easier now-a-days, from abroad, to supply the people with the produce of the surface than to maintain them in their position if denied the minerals below the surface. From these considerations important conclusions may be drawn, though not perhaps the conclusions drawn by the popular land-law reformers.

Two elements in the question of minerals are generally left out of view in discussing the question. The first is, that minerals cannot be worked out without injury to, and such disturbance of, the surface as to greatly lessen its value. The second is, that the minerals are extensively exported to the profit, not of the land-owner, but of the coal-master or iron-master. The object of the reformers would not be gained by nationalizing the coal and iron in (this part of) the earth, if they merely abolished the land-owner's royalty and left the coal-master and the iron-master with a profit correspondingly increased. On the footing of no confiscation, the land-owner would get his royalty whether the coal is worked out of his land by a coal-master or by the community. The person against whom the attack of the reformer has been chiefly directed would therefore lose nothing by the change, and so would appear to be now innocent of the accusations brought against him. If the abolition of royalties is not to happen, still they might be regulated and limited by law, and not left as at present to the decision of the land-owner, like the still more important question, whether the minerals shall be worked out at all, or left in the ground. On the coal sold for home consumption, or exported, several profits are gained which enter into the price. These profits are: the lordship or royalty paid to the landowner, the wages of the miner, the interest on the coal-master's capital, the return for the coal-master's services, and the commission of the merchant or middleman; to say nothing of carriage by land or sea, which occurs in every case, and way-leaves below ground and above ground, which have to be paid in some cases.

In any new and improved system that would please the reformers, which of these profits is to be stopped? The royalty cannot be withheld, the miner's wage must be paid, the capital invested must get its return, management must be paid for—whether the manager be the State or a coal-master—middlemen will not work for nothing, railways and ships must be paid for carrying, and B cannot be expected to give free passage through or over his land to the coal wrought out of the lands of A. But suppose the reformer did persuade Parliament to stop one or more of these profits which at present enter into the price of coal, who is to benefit by the stoppage? Will the coal consumed at home be sold cheaper, and will the coal exported maintain its price? And how will the difference between the prices of home-used and exported coal be dealt with? Questions like these must be faced and answered before "mining royalties" can be handed over to the reformers whose prescription is "abolition pure and simple." Unless Parliament is prepared to forbid the exportation of coal, in order that the people may buy cheap in a glutted market, or to permit exportation at a higher price, but take for the people the difference between the two prices, it is not easy to see how the nation is to gain by the abolition (or other changes), though it is easy to see who would suffer.

Except in rare cases, mining royalties are so small in amount as to fall far short of being worthy of the notice they have obtained in some quarters. But, whether large or small, they are fixed by the common law of market rates based on supply and demand. The land-owner cannot obtain more than the coal-master will give, and the coal-master will not give more than the mineral is worth in view of its situation and character. From all which, and confiscation being out of the question, we draw the conclusion that there is not much amiss with the present system, but only that a land-owner who should refuse to allow his minerals to be wrought might with justice be forced to grant a lease of them to a tenant on terms approved of by the Land Court. In other words, we would put his minerals on the same footing as the surface; and without injury to his patrimonial interests, we would compel the land-owner to make the coal, iron, and stone in his land available to the generation that wished, and was prepared to use them, on equitable conditions. This may seem a poor and lame conclusion if brought into contrast with the sweeping recommendations of some reformers; but, in view of all the circumstances, it is as far as we can go with a due regard to rights which it is impossible to infringe without doing more harm than good. The same reasons which were given at an earlier stage against undoing the arrangements of our ancestors regarding ownership of the surface apply to the proposal to impinge upon the royalties. But the attack is of far less public importance here than in the case of the surface, for it is not the royalty that makes coal dear. The sum per ton (which the land-owner gets) bears a small proportion to the sum that goes to the coal-master as interest on capital and return for management and profit. We have not heard of many land-owners, who bought their estates, making rich from mineral lordships, even when added to agricultural rents; we mean land-owners who bought their properties at market prices. But we are familiar with coal-masters and iron-masters amassing fortunes in the prosecution of their lawful calling. Yet it is curious that their gains have never been challenged, except in the form of strikes which seem to leave things where they were, and are even said to put money into the pockets of the masters. Joint stock or co-operative land-owning was lately (24th October, 1894) made the subject of a conference in the Holborn Town Hall. Why not joint stock coal-mining? Perhaps the main objection to such a system of dealing with our minerals might be that, while as much capital (perhaps more) would be employed and seeking a return, there would be more persons to be paid for management, and the public would not get coals cheaper than hitherto. Robbing Peter to pay Paul has never been thought good business; and robbing Peter without paying Paul has still less to recommend it. You would have to take more from Peter Proprietor than he possesses before you could put Paul Public in a prosperous position. If land could be got, like other things in the hands of owners, at market value, there would be no monopoly, and free trade in land would have dawned. Our scheme gives the freest trade in land that is possible without confiscation. If more is wanted, it must be got by robbery which can hardly be included in any list of reforms. Once we begin to rob the land-owners, the unsatisfied receivers of the plunder will pass on to other owners of other kinds of property, and will have no great difficulty in pointing out the element of unearned increment attaching to each kind in its turn. The plunderers will always be more numerous than the plundered, until the process has gone far enough. Till then it will be possible to obtain majorities in favour (not, of course, of plunder, but) of securing justice for the people at the expense of a few of the people. But "then," when only a disreputable minority wishes to plunder a majority now on the defensive, the *vox populi* will sound a new war cry, which will be the old cry come back again, "the rights of property." The majority, enjoying and defending its property, will probably lecture the insurgent minority, and seek to persuade them that the fault is not in the system, but in themselves. And, if classical authors have not gone out of fashion, the minority may even be reminded of the words of Cassius—

> The fault, dear Brutus, is not in our stars,
> But in ourselves, that we are underlings.

The insurgent minority is the trouble. Certain platform reformers who revel in statistics would have us believe that this minority is the majority. But it isn't. Most of those who are poor know that their position has more chance of improvement if they work and live soberly than if they are idle or intemperate and trust to agitators to raise them by reforms in the law.

Chapter XXI.

THE LAND AND POPULATION.

This Land Question has, for anyone who discusses it, the unhappy quality of being related to almost everything. It is obviously in close relation with the question of population. The existence of people on the land is a condition precedent, as we have seen, of its value. But when the people are numerous enough to crowd the land, and when by competition amongst themselves they have raised the value of the land, they begin to say it is all a mistake, and that the whole value beyond prairie value belongs to themselves. And then they want to cancel all the contracts by which, through long ages, their ancestors and they have raised the value of the land, and to take back the land at a price that would ruin the unfortunate land-owner who bought and paid for his estate. As for the owner who inherited his property, and who on the faith of the income learned no trade, business, or profession, he could drive a cab, and, if too old, he could go to the poorhouse. Now, this growth of the population is at once a good thing and a bad thing, in view of the Land Question. The sense in which it is a good thing by raising values is obvious, and has already been indicated, if not discussed. The sense in which it is a bad thing is not so much on the surface. Growth of population in the country, up to the point that the soil and trade and commerce of the country can support, means prosperity and proper development of resources. Growth of population beyond that point means undue competition, reduction of wages, armies of "unemployed," poverty, disease, crime. Then the philanthropist wails, and the reformer propounds his remedy. Curiously enough, the reformer is mad against the overcrowding of houses, but refuses to see any overcrowding of the country. With him emigration is deportation, and "clearances" are cruelties. "Surplus population" is a phrase that, for him, contains a heresy. In the opinion of some reformers, who deal only with abstract principles and men in the mass, everybody should "sit up" in the omnibus to make room for the extra passenger, and for as many extra passengers as choose to enter, or as those already in may choose to introduce. And, when the fares come to be collected, if the extra passengers cannot pay theirs, those who first filled the coach must subscribe and pay for them. This is so comfortable an arrangement for the "extras" that we are not surprised their number seems to increase. It suits some constitutions.

This class is landless in two senses. They own no land, and they hardly find room in the country. They want to go in and possess the land—not the land open to them in new countries, but the land in this country already reduced to possession by others. Human nature being what it is, there is no wonder that discontent follows poverty and envy discontent; and we know that envy, malice, and all uncharitableness are a trio that keep company together. When these characteristics of mankind are left out of view by reformers, with their abstract principles and men-in-the-mass theories, it is easy to see how land reform by simple confiscation finds favour with so many who are incapable of understanding the subject but are attracted by the hope of easy gain. The "reformers" are also landless, and any property they possess would not be affected by their reforms. It would be some guarantee of the reformer's proposals if even a few landowners could be got to favour them; but the reformer will tell us that this is too severe a test. A similar test has not been found too severe in some other matters, for men are often to be found sacrificing their pecuniary interests for the sake of right and justice. But society cannot afford to remake its plans as often as, and simply because, there exists a number of people who are poor and uncomfortable under, but not by reason of, these plans. If the plans were equitable when they were made, the emergence of impecuniosity, even on a large scale, would not discredit the plans any more than the bankruptcy of a merchant is an impeachment of our system of commerce. Merchants sometimes ruin themselves, to say nothing of others, by trying to do too large a trade for the capital they own or can command.

The population question is too vast for discussion here, but we may glance at its bearing on the Land Question still a little further. We admit into this country any number and almost every class and condition of people who choose to come, whether they have anything or nothing. We permit marriages between persons who can barely maintain themselves when single and both wage-earning, though we know that the woman when she becomes a wife will cease to earn anything, and will, in all likelihood, become the mother of children whose very existence will reduce the parents to poverty and wretchedness. We admit food stuffs from every part of the world and products of handicraft of every sort "made in Germany" or anywhere else, all duty free, though by doing so we reduce farm produce at home below the paying point, and take the work out of the hands of our own artisans. When the inevitable result follows—farm rents falling and unpaid, land-owners barely able to pay the interest on their mortgages, the prices obtainable for home-made articles reduced, by foreign competition, to just a fraction above the cost of production, working people so underpaid as to be scarcely able to live, tens of thousands unemployed, pauperism increasing, charity unable to cope with the general distress—when all this happens, the surplus population sits still and the reformer flees to the unearned increment, land values, and what not, to put everything right. These causes of the trouble may be things which ought to be, or things which ought not to be. On that we offer no opinion here. But the proposed remedy we declare to be no remedy, but only a delusion—however honest the deluders and the deluded may be.

Chapter XXII.

THE LAND AND THE GAME.

GAME is one of the subjects that lie alongside the Land Question. By modern legislation it has been removed from the rank of burning questions, but it has not been, and cannot be, detached from the Land Question. In regard to game, farmers have now little to complain of, and they have ceased to complain except, in some cases, of the damage they sustain from the hunting of game. Some extreme advocates of the rights of the people will have it that wild birds and animals cannot be the property of man, and therefore should belong to any man who traps or kills them. That is the rule on the prairies, and the prairie argument, as we have seen, has fascination for some reformers. Here, again, abstract principles are more easily propounded than applied. If we could restore our country to the regretted glories of prairie and primeval forest, we would escape the difficulty of the game question rather than get over it. As it is, land first principles are not quite applicable to advanced stages of land cultivation and national progress. We have allowed the land to become private property, and we appear to be unable to undo this part of our past. Certain consequences, as we have seen, follow from the system of private property in land, and we may now glance at these as they affect game.

It cannot be said that game is attached to the land, and it must be admitted that game cannot be separated from the land. Our law gives the land-owner no right to follow a pheasant from his own field to the land of a neighbouring proprietor. When the bird crosses the march, and the land-owner is left lamenting, he may, pointing to the neighbouring proprietor, say, "Twas mine, 'tis his," but he must stop there, for it has not "been slave to thousands." The right is the right to kill, and keep when killed, or to trap, and tame when trapped. This right is confined to the owners of the land and their lessees, and is denied to the public. Land-owners and tenants of shootings find it necessary to employ gamekeepers to keep the public, in the form of poachers, in check, and the law defends the right and punishes the infraction of the right. It is almost idle to discuss the game rights of land-owners, for if these rights were given to the public there would soon be no game in the country. In the nature of the case, the quantity of game is limited by the area of the land, and even with the fostering care of the gamekeeper the quantity is seldom enough, and never too much, for those who have the right to kill it under present arrangements. Game is oftenest regarded from the point of view of the sportsman, but game, when killed, is food. To put an end to sport by extirpating the game would be a loss to many—to some, of their occupation, and to more, of their chief enjoyment. But in respect of these two classes the evil could not be called a serious national loss. To extirpate game as an article of food would be a serious loss to the people, and would be as foolish as to abolish the close time needed for breeding. As the number of guns must thus be limited, it seems natural and proper to put them in the hands of the land-owners and those deriving right from them. In other words, the present law does not seem to need reform in this branch. What has been said of game applies so much to rights of fishing that these rights hardly call, here at least, for separate consideration.

CHAPTER XXIV.

PRIMOGENITURE AND ENTAIL.

PRIMOGENITURE was mentioned at an earlier stage, but not more than mentioned. The subject is related to, though not absorbed in, the Land Question. Primogeniture is one feature of our law of succession, but it calls for notice here only as part of the Land Question. Under the present land laws the succession of the eldest son, and the effect of his succession in maintaining landed estates intact, have called forth the loud and vehement condemnation of reformers. Primogeniture obstructs commerce in land, and is thus an obstacle in the way of progress. It is therefore not surprising that the abolition of primogeniture has been talked of for a long time. The injustice of the rule has been recognised in questions between the heir-at-law and the other members of the family, and the rules as to collation were framed to mitigate the injustice. In the cases, however, where primogeniture produces the greatest inequality, and presumably the greatest injustice, collation is least effectual in adjusting the balance. The option to collate being given only to the heir, he makes hotch-potch of his inheritance and of the moveable estate with his brothers and sisters only when, by doing so, he either gains something or sacrifices very little. Collation has therefore left primogeniture very much where it found it, but we think the power of compulsory purchase, which is the leading feature of the reform here advocated, would destroy primogeniture, so far as the public is interested in it as part of the Land Question. It would matter nothing to the people whether the estate of a deceased landowner went intact to his eldest son, or equally among the whole children of the late owner. In both cases alike, the community would be able to supply their needs in land at market rates.. In course of time, when land-owners found that it was not land but income from land that they could confer upon eldest sons, these owners might begin to shrink from allowing, and still more from ordaining, a distribution so manifestly unequal and inequitable. The inequality and inequity (some would say iniquity) of primogeniture would become more palpable to land owners when they found that, even by sacrificing their younger children to family pride, they could not make sure that their ambition would (*post mortem*) be gratified. Under the proposed powers of compulsion it would depend, not on the will of the land-owner making his settlement on the lines of primogeniture, or, by intestacy, allowing the law of primogeniture to operate, but rather on the surroundings of the land itself whether the heir should continue to be a land-owner or become the mere sole possessor of an income from land in the shape of rents and feu-duties—in some cases an extensive first bondholder.

Entail is also, in its relation to the Land Question, entitled to greater notice than it has received above. Much that has just been said of primogeniture applies with equal, and perhaps greater, force to entail. But as entail is a crumbling institution which has suffered from the frequent attacks of modern legislation, we may, without pausing over entail, pass on to disentail. It is very surprising that those who urge on, and those who lead, the attack on the House of Lords should not make disentail the chief weapon of assault. Very few object to the House of Lords merely because it is a second chamber, but very many object to it on account of the hereditary principle in virtue of which a majority of the lords are legislators. Peerages are, somehow, linked with land, and are apt to become speedily extinct when peers become landless. It is entail, more than good management or anything else, that keeps landed estates in particular families either of lords or commoners. The surest, if not the quickest, way to abolish the hereditary legislator is therefore to abolish entail, or introduce easier means of disentail. Abolition would be the surest. Disentail would operate, we fancy, as a weeding process both of great land-owners and of hereditary legislators, and would leave the second chamber in the full strength of its members who were sent up by their country, rather than sent down by their progenitors, and of such of its members, if any, as had withstood the weeding process. But this is not the Land Question, though perhaps first cousin to it, so we shall have to be content with these by-the-way observations on the House of Lords and its amendment.

If the compulsory taking of land which we propose were made lawful, entail would lose its sting in regard to the Land Question. All that would remain would be the concentration in a few pockets of large incomes from land, which might have done more good if divided on the principles of moveable property. That, however, would be a question of a different sort from the Land Question, and would, no doubt, receive due consideration on its own merits, though we cannot follow it here. Abolition of entail would not break up, it would only tend to break up, large estates. Those in remote corners, far from great centres, might be very little affected by the change in the law; but as these are not the landed estates out of which the Land Question arises, it would not matter much. Those estates, however, contiguous to growing towns would be gradually bought up in small lots till very much reduced, or perhaps extinguished, as landed properties. And as it is such estates, or properties, which give rise to the Land Question, the process of reduction or extinction of these estates would imply the solution of the Land Question, for the people would be getting all the land they wanted without paying more than market price. Abolition of entail is perhaps more than the reformer could expect within a short time, but enlarged powers of disentail should not be so much beyond his reach. At present the owner of entailed property, whether an institute or heir of entail, has powers of disentail more or less ample according as he was born before or after 1st August, 1848.

The alteration in the law which appears best to meet the circumstances of our time is the giving of power to the institute or heir of entail in possession, no matter when born, to obtain disentail without any consents at all, but only on giving compensation to certain of the next heirs. And it might be worth considering whether, if the owner in possession refused to disentail, the next two or three heirs, if agreed, should not be able to force disentail, except where the owner happened to be the institute of the entail, *i.e.*, the person who first possesses under the entail. Sometimes the institute is himself the maker of the entail, and in every case he is the person intended to take the first benefit under it. If the owner for the time being were the maker of the entail in his own favour, it would be robbing him of part of his own property to force disentail (with compensation) against his wish; but if he is owner by inheritance, he would only be sharing the inheritance with the other heirs if they forced him to sell and take his portion in cash. No doubt he would think himself ill-used, and would complain accordingly; but as he would get the value, in money down, of what he lost in rental, his

I

grievance would not be very grievous. The answer with which he would have to be satisfied would be that the heir in possession for the time being would always be able to prevent disentail if every heir was to be sheltered from what the present owner calls his grievance. And seeing that his ancestor, the maker of the entail, saw fit to give only a life interest to the grumbler, that gentleman should esteem himself happy in getting compensation, in cash down, on the basis of his living for a certain number of years for which he holds no lease of life. Either he must be left with his cause of complaint, or disentail must be made dependent on the man in possession. Public policy must prevail over private sentiment.

Chapter XXIV.

CASUALTIES OF SUPERIORITY.

SINCE renewal of investiture was abolished the "superior" has dropped from his ancient place and lost his ancient power, and is now, in regard to his so-called vassals, nothing more than a creditor holding a first bond over the feu. True, his bond carries right to certain perquisites, called "casualties of superiority," which fall in at odd times when he least expects and when the new vassal can least afford them. A reverence for the feudal system has led some (even ardent) reformers to formulate plans for the abolition of these casualties, but always on compensation. When Church Patronage was abolished patrons were allowed to claim compensation, but very few did claim. If twenty years were given to superiors in which to claim, and if the compensation were fixed as low as the character of the exaction would justify, it might come to pass that many superiors would not think it worth their while to claim, especially if the superior had to begin the proceedings, and more especially if the vassal had his choice between compensation by a single payment and compensation by an addition to the yearly feu-duty, and if the option were open to him up to the close of the period or proceedings. If it be said that these conditions show too little regard to the interests of the superiors, we may fairly reply: Not less than they show to their own interests in this respect in very many instances. The right is one kept alive by zealous factors and leisured law agents rather than by superiors themselves, who, to judge by the way in which they so often compromise their claims for casualties, are rather ashamed of them than otherwise. The reformer has wanted courage in dealing with this question, and that is perhaps why it is still unsettled. It would be difficult for even the antiquary to show what the superior gave for the right to exact casualties. The foundation of these exactions is such that one can have little respect for them except what is due to their venerable age. If they are hoary-headed, they are hoary-headed sinners. To sweep them away without compensation would be confiscation only in name, for even the modern purchaser of land will hardly dare to say that the casualties entered into his calculations when fixing the price he would offer or pay for the estate. As a growth of custom with no foundation either in contract or justice, casualties would have disappeared before the hostile views of lawyers and laymen had it not been for the power of superiors to keep the custom alive by exaction, without requiring to discuss the right. They had the title which, for some purposes, is better than the right. "Right, title, and interest" is a phrase which (amongst others) brings down upon lawyers the accusation of using several words to express the same thing. Perhaps the accusation is not always so well founded as those suppose who make it.

Casualties of superiority are the most unpopular feature of our land system, and the most irritating incident of the feudal system to those who have to pay casualties. They are due on the ("entry," that is the) coming into possession by an heir, who is liable for a year's feu-duty in addition to the feu-duty of the year in which he enters, and on the entry into possession of a purchaser (called "singular successor") who is liable for a year's rent in addition to the feu-duty of the year in which he enters. The payment from the heir is called relief duty; the payment from the purchaser is called composition. Neither of these exactions is payable where the entry is "taxed," *i.e.*, where the original feu-contract or feu-charter excludes the demand. Silence on the subject is held as leaving the superior in possession of his feudal rights of casualty. As feu-charters are drawn by the agent of the superior and only "revised" by the agent of the feuar (called "vassal"), it is not surprising that the feuar very seldom escapes the casualties. A sense of justice has caused the growth of a rule under which the feuar is allowed to deduct from the year's rent exigible from him, as the purchaser, certain allowances bringing down the gross rental to the nett rental. A fair consideration of these exactions is a necessary part of any discussion of the Land Question.

Such exactions are contrary to the spirit of the age if we may judge by the fact that modern feu-charters exclude them. Yet such is the tenacity of custom, and such the unwillingness of land-owners (or their agents) to give up any of the ancient advantages of land-owning, that, where casualties are excluded, an equivalent has frequently been introduced under the name of "duplicand." The duplicand is commonly a double feu-duty every nineteenth year. Where that has been specially bargained for, the reformer must let it alone, as we think; but where the casualties are exigible under common law, there is thought to be room for improvement in our system. The feus subject to casualties are mostly old feus on which the feu-duty is small. We cannot tell whether the superiors who gave off these feus accepted small feu-duties because of the right to casualties, but we should hardly think they did. A man seldom accepts inadequate present compensation on the faith of future and uncertain supplement. Even if precarious casualties entered into the rate of feu-duty, it is quite, or almost quite, certain that the casualties would be mentally calculated on the basis of then present prospects as to their amount. If we may take this assumption for our basis, it suggests a principle for the guidance of the reformer in regard to the commutation of casualties. That principle should be to refuse right to commutation on the basis of a higher rental, in the case of buildings, than was bound to be created for the securing of the feu-duty, in terms of the feu-charter, or was actually created within, say, five or ten years of the creation of the feu. In the case of land, the rental might be the rental at the date of feuing. If these suggestions are thought to be too hard on the superiors and too favourable to the vassals, we reply that it is just in this branch of our land laws that hardship is most felt, and that reform, on such moderate lines as we have ventured to lay down, will inflict the minimum of sacrifice consistent with any reform at all. It is not easy, it is not possible, to make reforms without changes less or more adverse to some interest, less or more repugnant to some party or from some point of view. Everybody is not pleased with things as they are: the least we can expect is that there will be fewer objectors to things as altered. In neither case, however, are objections to receive much consideration if founded only upon self-interest. Under our constitution there is not much danger of class self-interest dominating reform or securing its rejection. The greatest danger exemplified by contemporary history is the promising of reforms to secure votes, and the having to fulfil pledges in the teeth of reason and justice, if only the sufferers by the fulfilment are not too numerous.

But the multiplicity of reforms on which pledges are taken, though suggestive of no great earnestness on the part of the candidates who give the pledges, is a sort of guarantee that the reforms will not be pushed forward with the alarming swiftness indicated by the utterances of candidates for parliamentary honours. Members are usually more cautious than candidates, and "the House" is a better sedative than "the hustings."

Chapter XXV.

PRESCRIPTION, SEARCHES, AND RECORDS.

PRESCRIPTION, as applied to land rights, calls for some notice here. The law of Scotland is familar with various prescriptions, but it has reserved its greatest, called "the long prescription," for land. There may be wisdom, and clearly there is expediency, in requiring that a pretty long use—by the public, for instance—of a footpath shall precede the constitution of a right-of-way along that footpath. But it is not so obvious that it serves any good or public purpose to require the seller of a bit of land to produce or deliver to the buyer a prescriptive title running back for forty years. What is the theory of prescription as applied to titles to land, and what is the principle underlying it? It is "lest perchance" the man in possession on a written title should not after all be the true owner. However good in reality his right and his title may be, it is thought best not to call them good "lest perchance" someone else may come forward with a better right, which he had not been able to assert, or thought it worth his while to assert, for the trifling period of twenty or even forty years. The right of the purchaser in open market for a full price is kept in suspense for the prescriptive period "lest perchance" somebody who is unknown to the records should come forward and prove, in the language of the stage, that he is "the rightful heir." The chance may be what is familiarly called an off-chance, but the laws (and lawyers) delight in showing that sagacity and foresight which provide for all contingencies. It is pretty safe to assert that there are many conveyancers of large and long practice who never, in all their experience, found a right saved by prescription which would have been lost but for prescription. Yet the law of prescription is maintained, and is held in reverence by lawyers "lest perchance."

It is this law of prescription that renders searches a necessary part of every seller's title, and throws upon owners of land a good deal of additional expense in cases of transfer. In the absence of stipulation the seller bears the cost of searches, but, so obnoxious is the burden, exposers of property for sale by public roup frequently make it one of the articles of roup that, though they will discharge burdens disclosed by a search, the buyer must procure the search at his own expense. It is, of course, quite right that a buyer should obtain correct and reliable information as to the state of the title, but it is not right that such information should cost more than the trouble of reading the seller's document of title. The system we have recommended would antiquate the (positive) prescription of land rights and supersede searches, and cheapen the transfer of land, without in the least endangering the rights of buyer or seller. Except from the standpoint of the existing *régime*, it is difficult to imagine why the man who neglects a right to land should be more tenderly dealt with than the man who neglects a right to personal property. In ancient times there may have been good reasons for the distinction, but these reasons have long since ceased to exist, except in the mind, and begotten of the practice, of the feudal conveyancer. And what is in his mind is not so much an opinion as an acquiescence in an inherited view, which it was his part piously to adopt rather than critically to enquire into. "Lest perchance" has had its day, and should now give place to "yea verily."

In outlining the Land Register, we took it for granted that there would be only one Central Register for the whole of Scotland. But there may be reasons in favour of County or District Registers which we did not stay to consider. The first and chief requisite of the certificate of title would, of course, be reliability, and convenience in getting it would come next. There would be the question whether towns and cities should have registers of their own, or should be treated as parts of the counties in which they are situated. These matters are not matters of principle; and, though mentioned, need not be discussed here.

Chapter XXVI.

SOME EFFECTS OF PROPOSED REFORMS.

It may as well be remarked here as left to the critic to point out that, while seeking to abolish the feudal system, we have spoken of land-owners under the new system as continuing to "feu" off their lands. We may call it what we like, but when the owner who has power to use the land transfers that power to another, either for a sum down or for an annual payment, the transaction is a sale. It is quite indifferent whether we avail ourselves of the terminology ready to hand from the feudal system or invent new names better suited to the new system. A crater is still a crater, though the volcano be extinct. It seems convenient to call it feuing a piece of land when it is given away for an annual payment, and to call that payment feu-duty. But, as we do not propose to maintain any incidents of feus other than the feu-duty, it might quite fairly be objected that the transaction was not one of feuing at all. In that case another name could be found, and "sale for annuity" might not be the best, but it would have the merit of being correct and descriptive. There should be no duplicand and no casualties, and the seller should have, and should have nothing more than, the position and rights and remedies of a first bondholder.

Owners of land will have many objections to our scheme. They will think it hard, and perhaps unjust, not to be allowed to continue to do what they like with their own. But if they persist in this position in the face of the considerations already discussed, it will be hopeless to argue with them. Like people past praying for, they must just be left alone. Time will do what argument failed to accomplish. An owner forced to sell or feu for less than the land in question cost him—forced, that is, to transact at a loss—will protest against the law. But he will have been safeguarded at two points: he did not need to part with his land at all if it was not standing idle but was serving its proper purpose, and he was not asked to take less than he was getting, or less than market value. If, yet, he must lose by the compulsory transaction, the only ground of complaint left to him will be that the law has not allowed him to hold on till the community raised the value of his land for him by their (not his) action. If B holds a plot of ground adjoining the engineering works of A, and if that plot, from size, shape, and surroundings, is worth nothing, or next to nothing, to B or anybody else; is bringing in no income to B, and is even costing him £5 a year to hold it idle; and if A needs it for extending his works, how should A and B deal? The works cannot be extended in any other direction, except at prohibitive cost. Is A's extremity to be treated as B's opportunity? Unless B is allowed to exact from A the uttermost farthing which A will give rather than not extend his works, B will think himself aggrieved and the victim of a confiscatory law. Under that law as we propose to frame it, B would be saved his yearly loss of £5, and would even get for his ground the utmost price which immediate competition could secure. But the law would, without remorse, prevent him from making a victim of A. If there must be a victim, and apparently there must, the public interest demands the selection of B to the extent stated in the case supposed.

Bondholders are a very important class in relation to the Land Question. Any alteration of the law which would unsettle their rights and injure their position would have consequences reaching far beyond the conceptions of the casual observer. Individual lenders and private trusts seek heritable security when they look for first-class investments, but they are not so much concerned as, for example, insurance companies. It is easy, but not pleasant, to picture the ruin which would ensue from any change in the law to the prejudice of the securities obtained for the millions lent on land even by a single company. If it is a proprietary company, the shareholders might lose their share capital, but what about the life policy-holders and their widows and families? Perhaps the land restorationist has not thought of that. His reform, which he was willing to press even to the ruin of the men of whom it is the fashion to say that "they toil not neither do they spin," would have consequences for the toilers and spinners which it never entered into his heart to conceive. That, however, is nothing wonderful, for men who are carried away by what they call a "principle" which they do not understand will find themselves landed at results which they did not anticipate.

Chapter XXVII.

CONCLUSION.

Nothing is so subversive of sound reasoning as a foregone conclusion. Attachment to a view is too often synonymous with determination to maintain it against all comers and at all hazards. It even enables the devotee to shut one eye and see only with the other. Nay more, it enables him to misread the plainest of plain English, and to find in language what he would like it to express rather than what it truly contains. In May, 1887, the late Lord Chief-Justice Coleridge delivered an address to the Glasgow Juridical Society on "The value of clear views as to the laws regulating the enjoyment of property." For the last seven years that address has been a favourite authority with some land restorationists in support of their evangel. One of these reformers puts his case thus: "There are acres in Glasgow for which labour has to produce, for a private individual, £100,000 or about £5000 per annum before it can eat or drink. How can a living wage be paid so long as this oppression lasts? But the objection arises, will you take from these ground-owners property for which they have paid honestly-earned money? I answer—The public good is the supreme law: *Salus populi suprema lex est.* I quote

Lord Chief-Justice Coleridge addressing the Juridical Society in Glasgow. 'The history of these islands is full of examples in which the principle has been unhesitatingly applied to whole classes in the name of the public good. To corporations it has been constantly extended . . . made up of individuals who have had to submit to deprivation of property and consequent loss of position without a shadow of compensation.'" The impression here conveyed, and no doubt intended to be conveyed, is that the Lord Chief-Justice was on the side of the land restorationists and no compensation. But he wasn't.

The ordinary reader would be led to believe that this eminent jurist had pronounced, at Glasgow, in favour of "deprivation of property and consequent loss of position without a shadow of compensation." No doubt he gave two instances in which loss is not compensated, namely, where in time of war the general in command of our own soldiers orders the destruction of a house which, if left standing, might be an important military position for the invading army. The other instance his lordship gave in these words: " Parliament supplies the funds for a great public and national harbour, created by a huge breakwater which the officers of the sovereign construct. The effect of this great national work is to turn the tide of the sea full on to the lands of a beach-bounded proprietor some miles off, who could only save his land from utter destruction by the erection of a long and

K

massive sea-wall. Has he a claim, a legal right, to compensation? Again I answer, most certainly not. *Salus populi suprema lex.*" These are very different cases from the one to which the restorationist, as we saw above, proposed to apply "the principle" in favour of which he quoted disjointed passages from the Lord Chief-Justice. The proposition which his lordship was seeking to establish by the paragraphs from which the quotations were drawn was that "you may no doubt alter the laws of property on a proper case being shown for the alteration," and that the State has both the right and the power "to deal with the common stock with or without compensation," and then he gave the two illustrations, both of which we have mentioned. But the learned judge went on to say " that any change in the tenure of property made by law should be made with as little suffering to individuals as may be, and with as much consideration as possible for the present holders and present expectants of property whether real or personal. . . . Men to whose personal loss the law is altered are, as matter of common fairness, to be considered in every way, and nothing should be done to their detriment which it is possible to avoid. Every one will agree with this." Having laid it down that the measure of compensation cannot be left to the party compensated, the Lord Chief-Justice went on to say, "We may assume that, as a rule, no changes in the laws of property or the conditions of its enjoyment are likely to be made, or ought to be made, except either with the consent of persons affected by the change, or with compensation, if his assent is not given." Once more: " It is very true that all change, or almost all change, of the laws of property affects either existing rights or rights which reversioners might naturally regard as certainly coming to themselves. This is a reason why, as I have already said, every such change should be made with care and tenderness, without unnecessary disturbance, with compensation satisfactory, if it may be, even to the persons unfavourably affected by the change, and doing no violence to the great principle that right must not be compassed by wrong, nor evil done that good may come of it. But it is not wrong to change the law on good reason and fair terms; it is not evil to vindicate the supremacy of the State over that which is being employed for its destruction."

The "clear views" which the Lord Chief-Justice was at so much trouble to recommend do not seem to be prevalent with land restorationists, who appear to be enamoured of a single principle to the utter disregard of all other principles. Justice is done by taking the whole facts and the complete case (whatever it may be) into consideration, and it is not safe to judge a "principle" taken *per se* and without reference to other principles as well established as that which, for the moment, is being held up as the *regula regulans* of the matter in hand.

PRINTED BY
WILLIAM HODGE & CO
GLASGOW.

www.ingramcontent.com/pod-product-compliance
Lightning Source LLC
LaVergne TN
LVHW081353060426
835510LV00013B/1807